Mastering New Testament Facts

| PROGRAMMED READING |
| ART AND ACTIVITIES |
| TESTS |

to get it all down PAT

BOOK 2
The Fourth Gospel and Acts

Madeline H. Beck
Lamar Williamson, Jr.

Sketches
MARTHA WILLIAMSON

JOHN KNOX PRESS
ATLANTA

Second printing 1976

International Standard Book Number: 0-8042-0327-X
© John Knox Press 1973
Printed in the United States of America

PREFACE

Mastering New Testament Facts is a guide for both individual and group study of the New Testament. While it has been designed for individual use, it is also easily adapted for use by study groups or classes.

Suggestions for Individual Study

The approach followed in *Mastering New Testament Facts* is one which uses recently developed learning methods. Some of these may seem to be unfamiliar at first, even though they have been used successfully both in public school education and in industry. For example, the suggestion that the student take a pre-test before he has begun to study certain chapters may seem to be an unnecessary or perhaps even an unfair step. However, it has been found that a pre-test on unfamiliar material is often helpful. Pre-tests serve to alert the student to key questions. They are basically previews which help the reader learn the material faster. All of the techniques used in this study are ways of preparing or reinforcing one's memory.

It is very important for the student to read each set of instructions carefully. If the instructions should occasionally seem to be unclear, he might wish to share his questions about them with other students or with a teacher. As this volume has not been designed as a commentary or an interpretation of the theology of the New Testament, the reader may wish to supplement it with such resources as *The Layman's Bible Commentary, The Interpreter's Bible,* a good Bible dictionary, or an atlas. *Good News for Modern Man* (Today's English Version) is the most helpful translation of the New Testament to use with *Mastering New Testament Facts*. However, other versions of the New Testament may be used if *Good News for Modern Man* is not available.

Suggestions for Group Study

There are a variety of ways in which *Mastering New Testament Facts* can be used in group study, and each group is encouraged to work out its own procedure. The following ideas may offer suggestions.

1. Each participant in the study should have his own copies of *Mastering New Testament Facts* and *Good News for Modern Man* (Today's English Version).

2. The leader or chairman should help the participants with directions in the book that might not seem to be clear.

3. Regular opportunities for individual study should be included. Thus a class may agree for the individual study to be done outside of the class time. In this case, an agreement or covenant may be adopted regarding the amount of time to be spent or the amount of material to be covered. Other groups may discover that they work best by the concentration of individual study at one class meeting and the use of alternate meeting periods for general discussion. A third approach might be to use approximately the first half of each class period for individual work and the remaining half for discussion.

4. In order to stimulate discussion, the participants could mark on scratch paper or in the margins of their New Testaments the ideas in the passage that seem to be important. A class can devise its own symbols for marking these ideas. These could be quite simple, such as E--exciting, P--puzzling, D--disturbing, H--helpful.

5. If the class is large, it might be wise to divide it into groups of fifteen or fewer for discussion.

6. The discussion may be quite informal and free flowing. On the other-hand, it could be slightly directed. Some classes may wish to discuss first the ideas which seem to be exciting or helpful; others may wish to turn to those which are troublesome as a way of beginning the discussion.

7. The interpretation of a passage of Scripture is often related to particular concerns faced by the church at critical times in its history. Thus the class may enjoy discussing the meaning of a passage for earlier generations. It may also wish to discuss the bearing a passage has on situations faced today in the church, community, or world at large.

8. If the meaning of a particular passage remains difficult to grasp, someone in the class may wish to look for additional resources or further information.

9. Ideas which may work well with one class may not work at all with another. Therefore, each class should feel free to develop its own use of the book, realizing that it should balance discussion with time for individual study.

ACKNOWLEDGMENTS

The development of this course was made possible by the generous support of the Presbyterian School of Christian Education in Richmond, Virginia. President Charles E. S. Kraemer and Dean Malcolm C. McIver, Jr., made staff time and materials available and supported the project with their interest and encouragement.

The outline of the Gospel of John used here is adapted from that of Raymond E. Brown in *The Gospel According to John*, The Anchor Bible, vols. 29 and 29A (Garden City, N.Y.: Doubleday, 1966 and 1970).

Professional readers of portions of the course included Prof. James P. Martin, Miss Gay Mothershed, Miss Peggy Ross, and Prof. Richard N. Soulen.

Volunteers for trial testing of an early draft included students at P.S.C.E., Union Theological Seminary in Virginia, Randolph-Macon College, the University of Richmond, Virginia Commonwealth University, St. Catherine's School of Richmond, and members of Westminster Presbyterian Church, Richmond, St. Thomas Episcopal Church, Richmond, and Westover Hills Presbyterian Church, Little Rock, Arkansas. Mrs. Annette Dew of Richmond worked through all four books. Comments and suggestions from these readers and volunteers contributed greatly to the present form of the course.

Typists of original drafts were Sally Lockhart and Jane E. Miller of P.S.C.E. and Mrs. Ruth K. Parrish.

To all of these collaborators in the production of this course, the authors express their deep and genuine gratitude.

CONTENTS

BEFORE YOU USE THIS BOOK . . .

You can save yourself a lot of time by reading carefully the next three pages.

Description: This study guide to the New Testament appears in four books and has been designed to help you learn the content and structure of the New Testament in the shortest possible time. The books are:

> I. *Introduction and Synoptic Gospels*
> II. *The Fourth Gospel and Acts*
> III. *The Pauline Letters*
> IV. *The General Letters and Revelation*

All four books use the PAT system (Programmed reading, Art and activities, and Tests), which enables the student to get the facts down pat.

Uses: If you do the entire course, it will prepare you to interpret any part of the New Testament in the light of all the rest. It will provide the basic acquaintance with the New Testament which is necessary for an intelligent reading of scholarly works about the New Testament. It may be particularly helpful for church school classes or Bible study groups which seek a guide to the New Testament that leaves to the student full freedom of theological interpretation and historical perspective. Newly elected church officers, church school teachers, and candidates for ordination can use this course to review New Testament content.

Any one volume of the series will serve these functions for one portion of the New Testament. Specific objectives are listed at the beginning of each unit in the course.

Learning Process: Mastery of this material proceeds through five stages—one diagnostic, and four learning and evaluative. It is the student's responsibility to see that sufficient review takes place to ensure mastery at each stage beyond the first.

Stage 1: Diagnostic Unit Pre-test

Before you begin a unit of work, you will take a pre-test to measure your present mastery of the facts and skills taught in that unit, and to become acquainted with the types of questions and information you will be learning.

While a "pre-test" may sound strange, you will soon find that it is a help to you. It's not an evaluation but a way of learning, so don't be disturbed that you do not know the material. If you already know it, you do not need to study it.

By taking a pre-test, you will understand the objectives better, you will be more alert to the kinds of information you should remember, and you will have had practice in the kinds of questions you will be using for self-evaluation later.

Then, by comparing the results of your pre-test with those of a unit test after your study, you will be able to see just how much progress you have made by studying the unit. This growth is in knowledge only. The program does not attempt to provide for or measure any growth in faith or development as a Christian. It is up to the individual to use this information as he thinks best.

Stage 2: Guided Reading

You will be asked to read a chapter or so at a time in the New Testament. Outline headings of each book are given in larger type, with major divisions in ALL CAPITAL LETTERS and major subheadings Initially Capitalized. Learning these headings will facilitate your memory of the content of each book and your understanding of the structure and relationship of the parts. As you read the passage under one heading and answer the questions, you will be expected to remember the heading and the major facts in that section.

Drawings of houses and other structures represent the outline headings. As the first outline heading is introduced, the first level of a building, labeled with the heading, appears on the right side of the page. By following the construction of this building, you will learn the structure of the book.

Periodically you will be referred to a section chart and asked to complete a visual book outline, thereby seeing each passage in relation to the rest of the book.

As you read the passages, a series of questions will call your attention to the portions of text that you need to remember. You should silently answer these questions as you read. Answers appear on the back of each page of questions. It is not usually necessary for you to give the exact wording in order to be correct. These questions and answers are only to guide your study.

Sketches, which will help you remember the facts by emphasizing main ideas, accompany most answers in the guided reading. They also summarize the distinguishing features of some books at the end of the guided reading. Take time to associate the sketches with the material you have just read. They reveal more than words and are easier to recall.

Stage 3: Section Tests

Each fact, relationship, or skill that is emphasized in the guided reading or text will be tested in a section test. Section tests are organized into categories of facts to be mastered. You are given help in computing your scores for each category and for the complete test. As you complete the Unit Growth Record, you will see your progress in each area. If you score less than 90 percent on any part of the section test, you should review the relevant material in the study guide and in the New Testament.

Stage 4: Unit Test

When all sections have been completed at the 90-percent level, you are ready to begin the unit test. Once again you will be measured on your mastery of each fact, relationship, and skill taught in the sectional guided readings. You are given help in computing your scores for each category and for the entire test. By comparing your unit test score with your pre-test score you can easily determine your growth during the study of the unit.

Stage 5: Study References

Scripture references are given for all <u>unit test</u> answers. By checking the references for any items you missed on a unit test, you can complete your mastery of this unit's content. If you score less than 90 percent you should review any areas of weakness before proceeding to another unit. This does not apply if your growth from the pre-test was more than 70 percent.

NOTE: This course was designed to be used with *Good News for Modern Man: The New Testament in Today's English Version*, and its language is generally used. However, equivalent terms are used interchangeably to help you accustom yourself to terms you will meet in other books. (Examples: letter/epistle; general/catholic; mighty works/signs.)

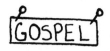

UNIT 1: THE FOURTH GOSPEL

OBJECTIVES

In Unit 1 the learnings have been classified in four major categories to
help you learn more easily and to know what you are learning. The four
categories are the same ones used in The Synoptic Gospels (Book I, Unit 2).

Upon completion of Unit 1, you will be able to do the following:

A. In the STRUCTURE category:

   State the major structural divisions of the Fourth Gospel.

B. In the NARRATIVES category:

   Associate at least 16 persons with the accounts about them in
   John's Gospel.

C. In the TEACHINGS category:

   1. State the seven "I am ..." sayings of Jesus.
   2. Identify four teachings found in John.

D. In the FEATURES category:

   1. Identify the probable circumstances, purpose, date of writing,
      and kind of authorship of the Fourth Gospel.
   2. Name the seven signs (mighty works or miracles) described in
      John.
   3. Name the four feasts mentioned in John.

In Unit 1, as in all units of this course, you are asked to take a pre-
test in order to help you learn. If you score 90 percent or more you may
move directly to Unit 2. However, most people will make a very low score
on the pre-test, since it is on material yet to be learned. Just taking
the test will teach you some facts, but its main value is that it will
center your attention on certain facts as you read the Gospel of John.
In addition, at the end of the unit you will have the pleasure of seeing
how much you have gained in factual knowledge.

Now begin the pre-test for Unit 1 on the next page.

PRE-TEST FOR UNIT 1:   THE FOURTH GOSPEL

A. STRUCTURE

Circle the letter of the ONE BEST answer for each statement.

1. The Gospel of John is divided into two major sections:
   a. The Galilean and Jerusalem ministries
   b. The Book of Signs and the Book of Glory
   c. The Word and the Book of Life
   d. The Word and the Passion
   e. Narrative and Discourse

2. Following the prologue, the FIRST major section has three subdivisions, the third being the climax of the section. The FIRST two subdivisions of the FIRST major section are:
   a. Preparation and Beginning Ministry
   b. Preparation and Feasts
   c. Feasts and Parables
   d. Beginning Ministry and Feasts
   e. The Word and the Signs

3. The SECOND major section has three subdivisions before the epilogue:
   a. Last Supper, Passion, Resurrection
   b. Feasts, Parables, Crucifixion
   c. Arrest and Trial, Death, Burial
   d. Little Apocalypse, Plots, Passion
   e. Prayers, Discourse, Crucifixion

4. The Gospel of John begins with:
   a. The birth of Jesus
   b. The Jewish hope of a coming Messiah
   c. The time before the creation of the world
   d. The call of the first apostles
   e. A genealogy

5. The Gospel of John ends with:
   a. The resurrection of Jesus
   b. A resurrection appearance by the lake
   c. The ascension of Jesus
   d. A warning
   e. None of the above

B. NARRATIVES

Persons. Circle the letter of the ONE BEST answer for each statement.

1. In John we read a description of the developing faith of:
   a. Nathanael and Nicodemus
   b. John the Baptist and Jesus' brothers
   c. Peter and Thomas
   d. a and c
   e. a, b, and c

6

2. Prayer, predictions to the disciples, and being anointed were three major ways in which Jesus:
   a. Prepared for his suffering
   b. Provided an example for his followers
   c. Taught the apostles
   d. a and b
   e. a, b, and c

3. At Lake Tiberias the disciples did ALL of the following EXCEPT:
   a. Ate bread and fish
   b. Sold their fish
   c. Had a fire
   d. Caught a lot of fish
   e. Saw the resurrected Jesus

4. When the soldiers came to arrest Jesus, he:
   a. Told them to put down their weapons
   b. Told his disciples to go home and wait
   c. Asked his disciples to stay with him
   d. Asked the soldiers to let his disciples go
   e. Asked forgiveness for the soldiers

Identify each of the following persons by writing the number of each name (right) on the blank of the term (left) most closely associated with that person. Use EACH name ONCE.

1. _____	God's messenger	1. Martha
2. _____	Spoke to Jesus at tomb	2. Jesus Christ
3. _____	The Word	3. Mary, mother of Jesus
4. _____	Doubted that the Messiah could come from Nazareth	4. Samaritan woman
5. _____	Attended a wedding	5. Thomas
6. _____	Picked up his mat and walked	6. John
7. _____	Born again	7. John the Baptist
8. _____	Reason for crowd at triumphant entry	8. Nicodemus
9. _____	Was asked for a drink of water	9. Nathanael
10. _____	High Priest	10. Simon Peter
11. _____	High Priest	11. Annas
12. _____	Provided for Jesus' mother	12. Adulteress
13. _____	Throwing the first stone	13. Caiaphas
14. _____	Doubted the resurrection	14. Mary Magdalene
15. _____	Sister of Lazarus	15. Man at pool
16. _____	You will never wash my feet!	16. Lazarus

C. TEACHINGS

Circle the number of the seven "I am ..." sayings found in John:

1. The Messiah
2. The bread of life
3. The Spirit of truth
4. The light to the Gentiles
5. The light of the world
6. The door
7. The wine of the soul
8. The good shepherd
9. The helper
10. The resurrection and the life
11. Living water
12. The way, the truth, and the life
13. The real vine
14. The gate to larger life

Circle the ONE BEST answer for each statement:

1. Jesus said he would draw all men to him:
   a. When he returned to the Father
   b. When he healed many people
   c. When he was lifted up
   d. If his disciples would believe and follow him
   e. As men saw his work

2. Jesus had told his disciples that troubles and persecution would come to them. He told them to be brave by remembering:
   a. His suffering
   b. His miracles
   c. The work of his church
   d. That he had accepted God's will
   e. That he had defeated the world

3. According to John, the Holy Spirit was seen as:
   a. A breath of life
   b. A dove from heaven
   c. Streams of living water
   d. a and b
   e. a, b, and c

4. Jesus gave his disciples a "new commandment" which John said was:
   a. To preach to all nations
   b. To love one another
   c. To believe in Jesus as well as in the Father
   d. To accept persecution for Jesus' sake
   e. To learn from one another

D. FEATURES

Background. Circle the ONE BEST answer:

1. The Gospel of John
   a. Is anonymous
   b. States that the author is the apostle John
   c. Does not state the name of the author in the text
   d. Honors John by being written in his name
   e. a and c

2. The Fourth Gospel appeared in its final form about:
   a. A.D. 40
   b. A.D. 60
   c. A.D. 80
   d. A.D. 100
   e. A.D. 200

3. John said he wrote his Gospel in order that:
   a. The disciples might have courage during persecution
   b. The world might learn about Jesus' life
   c. There would be an accurate record of Jesus' life
   d. Men might believe in Jesus
   e. Men might know what Jesus' teachings were

Special Content and Themes. Circle the numbers of the four feasts
mentioned in John:

1. Passover   5. Hanukkah
2. Pentecost   6. Tabernacles
3. Sabbath   7. Purim
4. Dedication   8. Feast of Lights

Now circle the number of each of the seven signs (mighty works) in John:

1. Feeding the 5,000   8. Healing lepers
2. Calming the storm   9. Healing the official's son
3. Raising Lazarus   10. Walking on water
4. Healing man at pool   11. Forgiving lost son
5. Healing paralyzed man   12. Teaching with authority
6. Raising Jairus' daughter   13. Healing man born blind
7. Turning water into wine   14. Obeying the Father

Check your answers on page 29 and compute your scores on the chart below
the answers. Then enter your percent scores on the Growth Record on
page 43.

UNIT 1: THE FOURTH GOSPEL

INSTRUCTIONS

You are about to begin the basic stage of the learning process in this course: guided reading. Unlike most units in the course, each of the two units in this volume concentrates on one New Testament book only. Unit 1 will guide your reading of the Gospel of John.

With only two exceptions (Mark in Book I and Philemon in Book III), these study guides follow the canonical order. In the canon John is inserted between the two volumes of the single work Luke-Acts. Therefore, John will be studied before Acts.

Although you would expect to read this unit straight down the page as in a normal book, after the introductory page the material has been written on divided pages as it was for the Synoptic Gospels (Book I, Unit 2).

This has been done to make it easier for you to learn. You will be able to concentrate on a small section at a time. You won't have to keep going back and forth to read questions, answers, and then questions again. Instead, you can move straight through the unit two times--top half, then bottom half. You should be able to remember all the questions on any half-page of text before you turn the page to check the answers--which might not be possible if you had to remember a whole page of questions.

The Gospel of John falls naturally into two major sections. The first section, the PROLOGUE and the BOOK OF MIGHTY WORKS, appears on the top half of the page, with headings numbered 11 and 12. The second section, the BOOK OF GLORY and the EPILOGUE, appears on the lower half of each page, with headings numbered 21 and 22. Subheads under these four main headings will be indicated by capital letters following the heading numbers and by initial capitalization of the subhead itself. For instance, the number 21A refers to the second half of John (2), the first major heading (1: THE BOOK OF GLORY) in that half, and the first subhead (A: The Lord's Supper) under that main heading.

In addition to the system of numbering and of capitalizing the headings, this unit will also use the symbolic building of a house, a factory, and a ladder to help you learn the structure of the Fourth Gospel. These three completed symbols are shown on the next page. You will "build" them level by level as you proceed through the outline of the guided reading.

You are being asked to memorize an outline of the Fourth Gospel in order to help you find passages in John and to remember its content. If you are familiar with a different outline and prefer to use it, you need not learn this one. You may simply substitute the one you prefer for the outline portion of the section and unit tests. However, very few people will have this background and most will find it advantageous to learn the outline given here.

AUTHOR: Anonymous (the author does not state his name in the text).
          Traditionally: The apostle John in Ephesus near the end of his
          long life.

DATE: Final form near A.D. 100.

READERS: Combination of Jewish, Hellenistic, and Gnostic traits point to a
          Hellenized Jew writing for a fairly sophisticated audience in the
          eastern Mediterranean basin.

PURPOSE: See 20:31. To win converts and confirm the faith of believers.

STRUCTURE
Below are visualizations of the structure of the Gospel of John as a whole
(the house), and of its two major parts: the Book of Mighty Works (the
factory) and the Book of Glory (the ladder). You will see portions of these
being built from the bottom up to help you learn headings as you work
through the guided reading questions.

(Turn page for questions on background.)

Circle the letter of the ONE BEST answer for each statement:

1. The author of the Fourth Gospel, as stated in the text, was:
   a. The apostle John
   b. John's disciple
   c. Unnamed (anonymous work)
   d. John Mark
   e. A school of writers

2. The Gospel as we have it was written about:
   a. A.D. 65
   b. A.D. 80-100
   c. A.D. 90
   d. A.D. 100
   e. A.D. 120

3. The readers were probably:
   a. Uneducated
   b. Jewish Gnostics
   c. Fairly well-educated people in eastern Mediterranean region
   d. People living in northern Galatia
   e. a and d

4. The Gospel of John was written to:
   a. Allay fears due to persecution
   b. Win converts to Christianity
   c. Record the life story of Jesus
   d. Confirm the faith of believers
   e. b and d

Check your answers with those at the bottom of this page. If you made any errors, reread the background information on page 11. Then go on to 11 on page 13, using the following procedure:

1. Note outline heading, and any description preceding the questions.

2. Read the questions on one half of one page to guide your Bible reading.

3. Read the Bible passage assigned.

4. Reread the questions and then try to answer them from memory. You need not write the answers unless you find this helpful.

5. Look at the Bible to finish answering the questions.

6. Then and ONLY THEN turn the page to check your answers. Get the sense of the answer; exact wording does not usually matter.

7. Note the drawings. They will help you remember the important points.

8. Fill in blanks in section charts as instructed from time to time.

9. If you like, do the optional Just for Fun activities that you'll find.

10. At the end of each half of the Gospel, take the section test. Check answers and review weak points.

11. Finally, take unit test. Look up references for questions you miss.

12. Fill in Growth Record on page 43 to see your growth in knowledge of John.

Answers: 1,c; 2,d; 3,c; 4,e.

11 PROLOGUE: THE WORD
READ: John 1:1-18

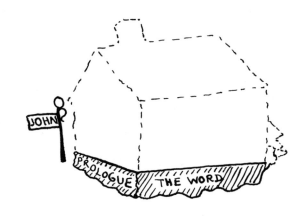

1. What part did the Word play in the creation of the world?

2. Who was God's messenger?

3. What did the Word become?

****

21 THE BOOK OF GLORY

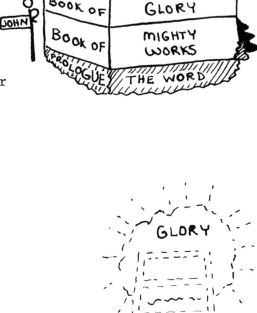

21A The Last Supper
READ: John 13:1-30

1. At the beginning of the last supper that Jesus shared with the Twelve, Jesus washed their feet.

   a. Who objected?

   b. Why did Jesus say he was washing their feet?

2. Jesus predicted that Judas would betray him. How did Jesus identify the betrayer to the disciples?

3. Does John's account of the Last Supper say anything about the institution of the sacrament of the bread and wine?

11

1. All things were
   made through him.

2. John

3. A human being

****

21A

1. a. Simon Peter

   b. To set an example

2. By dipping the bread
   in the sauce and
   giving it to him

3. No; he tells about the
   footwashing instead.

12 THE BOOK OF MIGHTY WORKS (signs)

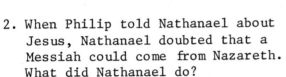

12A Witness of John the Baptist and His Disciples
READ: John 1:19-51

1. When Jesus met John, John called Jesus the Lamb of God. How did John know that Jesus was the Son of God?

2. When Philip told Nathanael about Jesus, Nathanael doubted that a Messiah could come from Nazareth. What did Nathanael do?

3. This passage tells how four men became disciples of Jesus. Can you list their names?

12B The First Two Mighty Works
READ: John 2--4

1. The <u>first sign</u> (mighty work) was given at a wedding in Cana. What was the sign and who requested it?

****

21A The Last Supper (continued)

After the supper, Jesus taught his disciples for the last time.

READ: John 13:31--14:31

4. What new commandment did he give them?

5. In the first part of his discourse--

   a. What did Jesus say he was? (The <u>sixth "I am ..."</u>)

   b. What did Jesus promise the disciples that the Father would give them?

   c. What did Jesus promise to leave with the disciples?

12A

1. He saw the Spirit come down like a dove and stay on Jesus.

2. Nathanael went to see if it could be true.

3. Andrew, Simon (Peter), Philip, and Nathanael

12B

1. Jesus turned the water into wine. Mary, his mother, had asked him to help.

****

21A

4. To love one another

5. a. I am <u>the way, the truth, and the life</u>.

   b. Another Helper, the Spirit of truth

   c. His own peace

16

12B The First Two Mighty Works

2. Nicodemus believed that Jesus was sent by God.

   a. Who was Nicodemus?

   b. What teaching of Jesus did he find hard to believe?

3. When Jesus saw the Samaritan woman at the well, he asked her for a drink of water.

   a. What did he say he could give her?

   b. How did he identify himself?

4. The <u>second sign</u> or mighty work found Jesus in Cana again.

   a. Who asked Jesus to heal his son?

   b. Where was the son?

****

21A The Last Supper (continued)

   READ: John 15--17

6. In the second part of the last discourse (John 15--16)--

   a. What did Jesus say he was?   (The <u>seventh "I am ..."</u>)

   b. What did Jesus say to give the disciples courage in suffering?

7. In chapter 17 Jesus prays for his disciples.

   a. For whom did Jesus pray in verses 9 and following?

   b. For whom did Jesus pray in verses 20 and following?

   c. For what reason did he ask that they all be one?

12B

2. a. A Jewish leader,
   a Pharisee

PHARISEE

   b. "You must be born again."

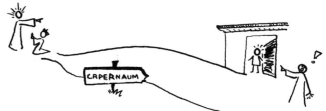

3. a. Living water

   b. As the Messiah

4. a. A government official

   b. In Capernaum

Turn to page 30 to study the chart of the beginning ministry and to identify Signs 1 and 2 by writing on the signposts what Jesus did. After checking your answers, turn back to page 19 to continue your study of the Book of Mighty Works.

****

21A

6. a. I am <u>the real vine</u>.

   b. I have defeated the world.

7. a. The ones God gave him;
      his disciples then

   b. Those who believe because
      of the apostles' message;
      his disciples now

   c. So the world would believe
      that the Father sent Jesus

THEN   NOW

Turn to page 31 to complete sayings 6 and 7. Check your answers on page 32, then continue your study of the Book of Glory on page 19.

JUST FOR FUN!! What did he say?

Try to put yourself in the place of the persons who lived or associated with Jesus. Try to think as they might have thought and conclude what they might have said or thought in response to one of the accounts in John.

Consider:

    a. Their backgrounds (as much as you know)
    b. Their limited knowledge (in science, medicine, psychology, etc.)
    c. Their probable personalities

What might each of the following have said?

1. The bridegroom when told: "You have kept the best wine until now."

2. Nicodemus to some Pharisees after his talk with Jesus

3. The Samaritan woman to her "husband"

(All Just for Fun activities are for interest only, not for testing. Any or all may be omitted.)

          ****

JUST FOR FUN!! There's something in a name.

A man's name is found in John and in Luke, but not in Matthew or Mark. In both John and Luke, he is sick and then dies.

After his death, one or more persons change their actions because of him. Yet, he is two different persons, a different individual in each Gospel.

What is this man's name?

(Answer is on next page. Don't look till you're ready!)

JUST FOR FUN!! Where is he?

Unlike the Synoptics, which tell of a long Galilean ministry and then
a short one in Jerusalem, John states four times that Jesus went to
Jerusalem. Indeed, most of Jesus' ministry as recorded in John takes
place in Jerusalem and Judea. Below is a record of his travels.

Bethany, across Jordan:
  1:19-42 (not to be
  confused with Bethany
  near Jerusalem)
Galilee: 1:43--2:12
Jerusalem: 2:13--3:21
Judea: 3:22--4:2
Samaria: 4:3-42
Galilee: 4:43-54
Jerusalem: Ch. 5
Galilee: 6:1--7:9
Jerusalem: 7:10--10:39

Judea: 10:40--12:11
  Across Jordan: 10:40-42
  Bethany: 11:1-53
  Ephraim: 11:54-57
  Bethany: 12:1-11
Jerusalem: 12:12--20:30
  In the city: 12:12--17:26
  Across Kidron: 18:1-12
  In the city: 18:13--19:16
  Golgotha: 19:17-37
  At the tomb: 19:38--20:18
  In the city: 20:19-30
Galilee: Ch. 21

What reason is usually given for Jesus' trips to Jerusalem?

         ****

JUST FOR FUN!!   There's something in a name.

The man's name is Lazarus.

In Luke: Lazarus is a begger with sores while alive. After death the
rich man from whom he used to beg sees Lazarus with Abraham, and asks him
to warn his brothers (Luke 16:19-31).

In John: Lazarus is the brother of Martha and Mary. He dies of illness
and is raised from death. Crowds flock around Jesus at the triumphant
entry because of the news of Lazarus being raised (John 11:1-44; 12:17-18).

12C The Feasts and Four More Mighty Works (chs. 5-10)
READ: John 5--6

1. The <u>third sign</u> (work) was given
   at Bethzatha (Bethesda).

   a. On which Jewish holy day (feast)
      did this occur?

   b. What did Jesus tell the man
      to do at the Sheep Gate?

   c. What did Jesus tell the man to
      do at the Temple?

   d. Why did Jesus say he had to
      work (heal) on the Sabbath?

2. The <u>fourth and fifth</u> signs took
   place during the Passover.

   a. What was the sign that made
      people want to force Jesus
      to be king?

   b. What was the fifth sign which
      frightened the disciples?

   c. What did Jesus say that he was?
      (The <u>first</u> "I am ...")

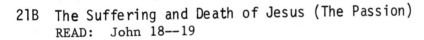

21B The Suffering and Death of Jesus (The Passion)
READ: John 18--19

1. When Jesus was arrested in the
   garden, what did he ask of
   the soldiers?

2. Jesus appeared before both the
   High Priest and his father-in-law.

   a. What were their names?

   b. Who fulfilled a prediction
      in the courtyard? How?

12C

1. a. The Sabbath

   b. Pick up his bed and walk

   c. Quit his sins

   d. Because his Father
      works always

2. a. Feeding the 5,000

   b. Walking on the water
      (Lake Galilee)

   c. I am <u>the bread of life</u>.

****

21B

1. To let his disciples go

2. a. Annas (father-in-law)
      and Caiaphas (High Priest)

   b. Peter, by denying
      Jesus three times

12C The Feasts and Four More Mighty Works (continued)
READ: John 7--9

Sign 6 was given after the Feast of Tabernacles.

3. Why did people say Jesus was not the Messiah?

4. What were the streams of living water?

5. What did Jesus say to the adulteress's accusers?

6. What did Jesus say he was? (Second "I am ...")

7. What was wrong with the man Jesus healed in Sign 6?

****

21B The Passion (continued)

3. When Jesus appeared before Pilate, he was found innocent. Pilate
   said he would free Jesus, but what did the Jews insist that
   Pilate do?

4. When Jesus was crucified--

    a. What did the notice on the cross say?

    b. How did Jesus provide for his mother?

    c. What happened when a soldier plunged his sword into Jesus?

5. Who prepared Jesus' body for burial?

12C

3. No one would know where
   the Messiah had come from.

4. The Holy Spirit

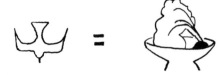

5. Whichever one of you has
   committed no sin may throw
   the first stone.

6. I am the light of the world.

7. He had been born blind.

****

21B

3. Free Barabbas and nail
   Jesus to the cross.

BARABBAS

JESUS

4. a. "Jesus of Nazareth, the
      King of the Jews" in
      Hebrew, Greek, and Latin.
      (See also Book I, p. 25.)

   b. He asked the disciple
      to consider her his
      own mother.

   c. Water and blood flowed
      from his side.

5. Joseph of Arimathea and
   Nicodemus

12C The Feasts and Four More Mighty Works (concluded)
READ: John 10

8. In what two ways did Jesus describe himself?
(The <u>third and fourth "I am ..."</u> sayings)

9. At the Feast of Dedication, what did the Jews say
was the reason they started to stone Jesus?

****

21C The Resurrection
READ: John 20

1. Mary Magdalene, Peter, and
another disciple found the
tomb empty. Who saw Jesus first?

2. Later, when Jesus appeared to
the locked-in disciples, how
did he give them the Holy
Spirit?

3. When Jesus appeared a week
later, Thomas was there.

   a. What had Thomas said he
   would need in order to
   believe the resurrection?

   b. What did he say when he
   saw Jesus?

4. Conclusion: Why was this
book written?

12C

8. I am <u>the door</u>.

   I am <u>the good shepherd</u>.

9. He was trying to make
   himself God.

Turn to page 30 to write on the blanks the names of the four feasts, signs 3-6, and sayings 1-4. Study the chart and check your answers on page 32. Then return to page 27 to continue your study of the Book of Mighty Works.

****

21C

1. Mary Magdalene

2. He breathed on them.

3. a. To put his finger
      where the nails had
      been and his hand
      in Jesus' side

   b. My Lord and my God!

4. That the reader might
   believe that Jesus is the
   Son of God and through this
   faith might have life

12D The Climax of the Mighty Works
READ: John 11--12

1. In <u>Sign 7</u> Jesus restored a dear friend to life.

   a. Who was the friend and
      the friend's family?
   b. What did Jesus say he
      was? (The <u>fifth</u> "I am ...")
   c. What did Caiaphas say
      should happen to Jesus?

2. Jesus prepared for the Passover
   and his death in three ways.

   a. Who anointed Jesus for
      his burial?
   b. Why did the crowd meet Jesus
      as he entered Jerusalem?
   c. When the Greeks wanted to
      see Jesus, what time did
      he say had arrived?

3. What did Jesus say would happen
   when he had been lifted up?

4. The Book of Mighty Works con-
   cludes with a summation of Jesus'
   ministry. After having been given
   the seven signs, how did most
   people respond to Jesus?

****

22 EPILOGUE: RESURRECTION APPEARANCES
READ: John 21

1. What did Jesus tell the
   disciples to do?

2. What was it that Jesus
   asked Peter three times?

3. What did he tell Peter
   to do each time?

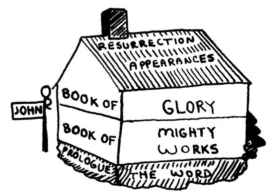

Conclusion: Jesus did much more
   than has been recorded.

12D

1. a. Lazarus, brother of
       Mary and Martha

    b. I am <u>the resurrection and
       the life</u>.

    c. He should die for the people.

2. a. Mary of Bethany
       (not Magdalene)

    b. Because they were impressed
       with his bringing Lazarus
       back to life

    c. The hour for him to be given glory

3. He would draw all men to him.

4. They did not believe him.

Turn to page 30 and complete all blanks on Section Chart 1. Check your
answers, review the corrected chart, and then take Section Test 1, page 33.

Turn to page 30 and complete all blanks on Section Chart 1. Check your
answers, review the corrected chart, and then take Section Test 1, page 33.

****

22

1. To throw their net out on
    the right side of the boat

2. Do you love me?

3. Take care of (feed) my lambs (sheep).

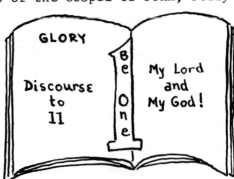

23 To remember the major sections and features of the Gospel of John, study
    this diagram:

The Word

MIGHTY WORKS
7
{ I am }
Feasts

GLORY
Discourse
to
11
Be One
My Lord
and
My God!

Turn to page 31 to complete the five remaining blanks in the Book of Glory
chart. Check your answers on page 32. After correcting your answers and
studying the charts, begin Section Test 2 on page 35.

Turn to page 31 to complete the five remaining blanks in the Book of Glory
chart. Check your answers on page 32. After correcting your answers and
studying the charts, begin Section Test 2 on page 35.

A. STRUCTURE (5)   **B. NARRATIVES (20)**

1. b	1. d	1. 7	6. 15	12. 6
2. d	2. a	2. 14	7. 8	13. 12
3. a	3. b	3. 2	8. 16	14. 5
4. c	4. d	4. 9	9. 4	15. 1
5. b		5. 3	10. 11	16. 10
			11. 13	

C. TEACHINGS (11)   **D. FEATURES (14)**

C. Teachings:

2	8	1. c
5	10	2. e
6	12	3. e
	13	4. b

D. Features:

Background
1. e
2. d
3. d

Special Content/Themes

Feasts:	Signs:	
1	1	9
3	3	10
4	4	13
6	7	

PRE-TEST SCORES FOR UNIT 1

Write the number correct for each category on the blank in the # column. Follow directions for finding the percent (using % chart below or multiplying as indicated) and write the percent in % column.

Category	# Correct		% Score	Directions
A. Structure	_____	=	_____	# correct times 20 = %
B. Narratives	_____	=	_____	# correct times 5 = %
C. Teachings	_____	=	_____	Check % chart below
D. Features	_____	=	_____	Check % chart below
Total (A+B+C+D) (Maximum possible: 50)	_____	=	_____	# correct times 2 = %

To find percent for C and D, circle the # correct in chart below. The number immediately below this number is the percent score.

C. Teachings

#	1	2	3	4	5	6	7	8	9	10	11#
%	9	18	27	36	45	55	64	73	82	91	100%

D. Features

#	1	2	3	4	5	6	7	8	9	10	11	12	13	14#
%	7	14	21	29	36	43	50	57	64	71	79	86	93	100%

Enter your percent scores on the Growth Record, page 43. Then begin your study of Unit 1 on page 10.

SECTION CHART 1

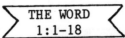

THE WORD
1:1-18

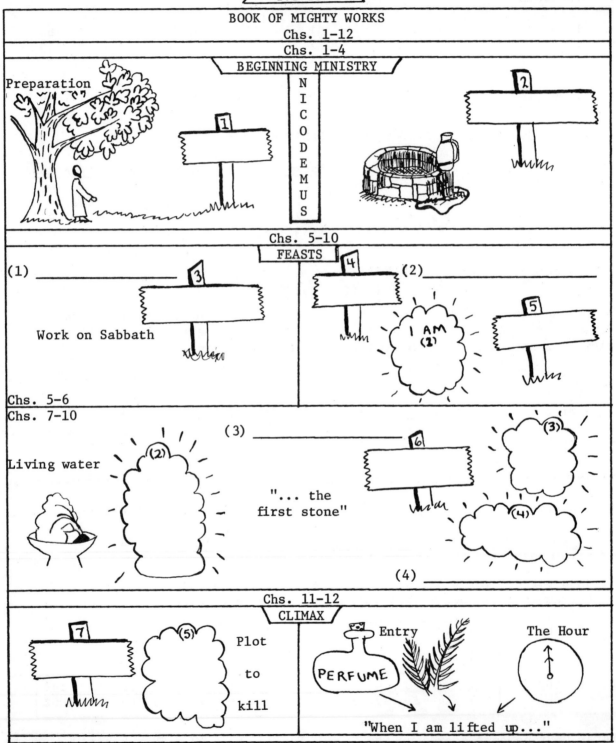

BOOK OF MIGHTY WORKS
Chs. 1-12

Chs. 1-4

BEGINNING MINISTRY

N
I
C
O
D
E
M
U
S

Preparation

1

2

Chs. 5-10

FEASTS

(1) _____

3

4

(2) _____

5

Work on Sabbath

Chs. 5-6

Chs. 7-10

Living water

(2)

(3) _____

6

(3)

"... the
first stone"

(4)

(4) _____

Chs. 11-12

CLIMAX

7

(5)

Plot

to

kill

Entry

PERFUME

The Hour

"When I am lifted up..."

Check answers on page 32.

BOOK OF GLORY
Chs. 13-21

Chs. 13-17

Chs. 13-14

Chs. 13-17

LAST SUPPER

Ch. 17

Acts:

6

Prayer:
ALL
BE
ONE
IN
GOD

Example

"Give you the Spirit"

13:36--16:33
Discourse:

7

Who?

Peace

"I have defeated the world"

Chs. 18-19

PASSION

Arrest

H (1) _____
I (2) _____
G
H

P
R
I
E
S
T
S

Trial

FREE BARABBAS

John and Mary

Buried by (3)_____

and (4) _____

Ch. 20

RESURRECTION

Empty Tomb

Breath of Life

Doubting Thomas believes:

Mary!

(5) "My _____ "

Book of John: To believe and have life

APPEARANCES
Ch. 21

Check answers on page 32.

ANSWERS TO GUIDED READING CHARTS

Seven  "I am" sayings of Jesus:

1. Bread of life

2. Light of world

3. Door

4. Good shepherd

5. Resurrection and
     life

6. Way, truth, and life

7. Real vine

Additional answers are as follows:

Section Chart 1

Seven mighty works (signs)
  1. Water into wine
  2. Healing official's son
  3. Healing man at pool
  4. Feeding the 5,000
  5. Walking on water
  6. Healing man born blind
  7. Raising Lazarus

Feasts:
  1. Sabbath
  2. Passover
  3. Tabernacles
  4. Dedication

Section Chart 2

High Priests:
  1. Annas (or 2)
  2. Caiaphas (or 1)

Buried by:
  3. Joseph of Arimathea (or 4)
  4. Nicodemus (or 3)

Thomas's affirmation of faith:
  5. "My Lord and my God!"

SECTION TEST 1

A. STRUCTURE.   Fill in the blanks to complete the following outline of
            Section 1:
   Prologue: (1) _____

I. The (2) _____

   A. Witness of (3) _____ and _____

   B. The First Two (4) _____

   C. The (5) _____ and Four More _____

   D. (6) _____ of the _____

In this section Jesus healed the official's son, the man at the pool, and
the man born blind. List the four other mighty works he did.

1. _____

2. _____

3. _____

4. _____

B. NARRATIVES

<u>Persons</u>.   Write the number of the person's name (right) before the phrase with
which it is most closely associated (left).   Use EACH name ONCE.

1. ___ Was at wedding with Jesus	1. Nathanael
2. ___ Met Jesus at the well	2. John the Baptist
3. ___ Doubted a Messiah from Nazareth	3. Nicodemus
4. ___ The Word	4. Samaritan woman
5. ___ God's messenger	5. Adulteress
6. ___ Told his friend about Jesus	6. Mary, mother of Jesus
7. ___ Accused by the Jews	7. Jesus
8. ___ Sister of Lazarus	8. Philip
9. ___ "Born again" saying hard to believe	9. Lazarus
10. ___ Raised from the dead	10. Martha

D. FEATURES

1. Circle the ONE BEST answer to the following statement:

Five of the "I am ..." sayings of Jesus appear in Section 1. They are:

    a. Love, life, light, truth, goodness
    b. Bread, light, door, shepherd, resurrection and life
    c. Bread, life, Son of God, living water, resurrection
    d. Light, shepherd, Messiah, truth, life
    e. Bread of life, wine of soul, Lamb of God, way, resurrection and life

List the four feasts mentioned in John:

2. _____

3. _____

4. _____

5. _____

Check your answers on page 41 and compute your scores below.

SECTION TEST 1 SCORES

Write the number correct for each category on the blank in the # column.
Follow directions for finding the percent score.

Category	# Correct	% Score	Directions
A. Structure	_____ =	_____	# correct times 10 = %
B. Narratives	_____ =	_____	# correct times 10 = %
D. Features	_____ =	_____	# correct times 20 = %
Total (A+B+D)	_____ =	_____	# correct times 4 = %

Enter your percent scores (for each category and total) on the Unit Growth
Record on page 43. Be sure to review the material for any items you missed.
Then turn back to page 13 to begin the study of Section 2, the Book of Glory.

SECTION TEST 2

A. STRUCTURE. Fill in the blanks to complete the following outline of Section 2:

II. The Book of (1) _____

    A. The (2) _____

    B. The (3) _____ and _____ of Jesus

    C. The (4) _____

    Epilogue: (5) _____

B. NARRATIVES

Persons. Write the number of the person's name before the phrase with which it is most closely associated. Use EACH name ONCE.

1. ____ Doubted the resurrection   1. Peter

2. ____ High Priest, father-in-law of High Priest   2. Jesus

3. ____ Protested foot washing   3. Annas

4. ____ Better that one man die for all   4. Nicodemus

5. ____ First to see resurrected Jesus   5. Mary Magdalene

6. ____ Identified by bread in sauce   6. Thomas

7. ____ Responsible for mother of Jesus   7. Pilate

8. ____ What is truth?   8. Judas

9. ____ Pharisee who buried Jesus   9. Caiaphas

10. ____ Did cooking at Lake Tiberias   10. John
         after crucifixion

C. TEACHINGS. Circle the ONE BEST answer to each statement:

1. The last two "I am ..." sayings of Jesus concerned:
    a. Real peace, and joy; and the vine
    b. The way, truth, and life; and the real vine
    c. The helper; and the way
    d. Love, hope, and joy; and the resurrection and life
    e. Eternal life; and truth

2. The Fourth Gospel describes the Holy Spirit as:
   a. A dove, fire, and tongues
   b. Fire and wind
   c. Wind and water
   d. Living water and rushing wind
   e. Dove, living water, and breath from God

3. John says Jesus offered courage to his disciples in his:
   a. Defeat of the world
   b. Love
   c. Obedience to the Father
   d. Example
   e. Sending of the Spirit

4. So that the world would believe him, Jesus prayed that:
   a. He would be resurrected.
   b. The world would understand.
   c. His followers would have courage.
   d. His disciples would be one.
   e. His church would live forever.

5. Jesus said all men would be drawn to him:
   a. As had been ordained from the beginning
   b. Because it was the Father's will
   c. When he was lifted up
   d. After his disciples had proved their faith
   e. By the power of the truth

Check your answers on page 41 and compute your scores below.

SECTION TEST 2 SCORES

Write the number correct for each category on the blank in the # column.
Follow directions for finding the percent score.

Category	# Correct		% Score	Directions
A. Structure	_____	=	_____	# correct times 20 = %
B. Narratives	_____	=	_____	# correct times 10 = %
C. Teachings	_____	=	_____	# correct times 20 = %
Total (A+B+C)	_____	=	_____	# correct times 5 = %

Enter your percent scores on the Unit Growth Record on page 43. Review any
work you missed. Then turn to page 37 and begin the unit test.

UNIT TEST 1

A. STRUCTURE

Complete the following outline of John by filling in the blanks:

Prologue: (1) _____

I. (2) _____

    A. Witness of (3) _____and His _____.

    B. The First Two Mighty Works (signs)

    C. The (4) _____and Four More Mighty Works (signs)

    D. (5) _____of the Mighty Works

II. (6) _____

    A. (7) _____

    B. (8) _____

    C. (9) _____

    Epilogue: Resurrection Appearances

List the seven mighty works or signs given in John, three of which are healing:

1.
2.
3.
4.
5.
6.
7.

B. NARRATIVES

<u>Persons.</u> Circle the letter of the ONE BEST answer for each statement:

1. John tells of the developing faith in ALL of these men EXCEPT:
    a. John the Baptist
    b. Nathanael
    c. Thomas
    d. Peter
    e. Nicodemus

2. Jesus washed the feet of his disciples because he wanted to:
   a. Purify the disciples
   b. Provide them an example
   c. Make them more comfortable
   d. Establish a ritual
   e. All of the above

3. Before going to the garden, Jesus prayed for:
   a. His disciples with whom he had lived
   b. All his followers through later ages
   c. Those who had died
   d. His enemies
   e. a and b

4. When Jesus appeared to the seven disciples at Lake Tiberias:
   a. He walked on water.
   b. He told them where to put their nets to catch fish.
   c. He built a charcoal fire and cooked for them.
   d. The disciples were frightened.
   e. b and c

Identify the following women in John's Gospel by writing the number of each
name (right) before the phrase with which it is most closely associated (left).
Use EACH name ONCE.

_____ Was told Jesus could give living water	1. Mary, mother of Jesus
_____ Asked Jesus to help at wedding	2. Martha
_____ Sister of Lazarus	3. Mary Magdalene
_____ No man accused her	4. Samaritan woman
_____ First to see resurrected Jesus	5. Adulteress

Identify the following men by writing the number of each name before the
term with which it is most closely associated. Use each number only ONCE,
except for Jesus, as indicated.

_____ The Word	1. Lazarus
_____ Went to see, in spite of doubt	2. John the Baptist
_____ A Pharisee who found one teaching hard to believe	3. Nathanael
_____ Called Jesus "Lamb of God"	4. Nicodemus
_____ Walked out of tomb	5. Jesus (use twice)
_____ Was identified as betrayer by bread dipped in sauce	6. Thomas
_____ Water and blood flowed from side	7. Disciple Jesus loved
_____ Took care of mother of Jesus	8. Peter
_____ Asked for proof of resurrection	9. Judas
_____ "You know I love you"	

C. TEACHINGS

Circle the letter of the ONE BEST answer for each statement:

1. Jesus gave the following reason for asking that the disciples be one:
   a. So that they would love one another
   b. So that his church would be one
   c. So that the world would believe
   d. Because God was one
   e. Because he loved them

2. Jesus said that when he was lifted up:
   a. Evil-doers would fall.
   b. The world would know him.
   c. He would return to the Father.
   d. He would draw all men to him.
   e. b and d

3. Knowing that he was going to suffer humiliation and a cruel death, Jesus told his disciples to find courage in:
   a. His acceptance of his Father's will
   b. His past works
   c. His defeat of the world
   d. The work of the disciples, then and in later years
   e. b and d

4. In John the Holy Spirit is described as:
   a. Tongues of fire
   b. A dove from heaven
   c. A breath from God
   d. Streams of living water
   e. b, c, and d

List the seven "I am ..." sayings as given in John:

1.

2.

3.

4.

5.

6.

7.

D. FEATURES

Circle the letter of the ONE BEST answer:

1. The stated purpose of the Gospel of John was that the readers:

    a. Might have life
    b. Might understand why the Jewish arguments were wrong
    c. Might believe in Jesus as the Messiah
    d. Might have courage in a time of persecution
    e. a and c

2. Some scholars think that a Hellenized Jew may have written this Gospel to sophisticated readers in the eastern Mediterranean basin because of ALL the following cultural influences EXCEPT:

    a. Jewish
    b. Greek
    c. Roman
    d. Gnostic
    e. Hellenistic

3. The Gospel's final form appeared about:
    a. A.D. 50
    b. A.D. 100
    c. A.D. 150
    d. A.D. 200
    e. A.D. 300

4. The four feasts at which Jesus performed signs and/or taught included ALL of the following EXCEPT:

    a. Passover
    b. Tabernacles
    c. Dedication
    d. Pentecost
    e. Sabbath

Check your answers on page 42 and compute your scores on page 43.

ANSWERS TO SECTION TESTS

Section Test 1

A. STRUCTURE (10 questions)

Outline (6)

1. Word
2. Mighty Works (signs)
3. John the Baptist and His Disciples
4. Mighty Works (signs)
5. Feasts and Four More Mighty Works
6. Climax of the Mighty Works

Works Other Than Healing (4)

1. Water into wine
2. Feeding 5,000
3. Walking on water
4. Raising Lazarus

B. NARRATIVES (10)

1. 6
2. 4
3. 1
4. 7
5. 2
6. 8
7. 5
8. 10
9. 3
10. 9

D. FEATURES (5)

1. b
2. Sabbath
3. Passover
4. Tabernacles
5. Dedication

Section Test 2

A. STRUCTURE (5)

1. Glory
2. Last Supper
3. Suffering and death
4. Resurrection
5. Resurrection appearances

B. NARRATIVES (10)

1. 6
2. 3
3. 1
4. 9
5. 5
6. 8
7. 10
8. 7
9. 4
10. 2

C. TEACHINGS (5)

1. b
2. e
3. a
4. d
5. c

ANSWERS TO UNIT TEST 1

A. STRUCTURE (16 questions)

Outline (9). (See pages 30-31, 33, 35.)   Signs (7). (See pages 30 and 33.)

1. The Word
2. Book of Mighty Works
3. John the Baptist and
   His Disciples
4. Feasts
5. Climax
6. Book of Glory
7. Last Supper
8. Suffering and Death
9. Resurrection

1. Water into wine (2:1-11)
2. Healing official's son (4:43-54)
3. Healing man at pool (5:1-18)
4. Feeding the 5,000 (6:1-15)
5. Walking on water (6:16-21)
6. Healing man born blind (9:1-41)
7. Raising Lazarus (11:1-44)

B. NARRATIVES (19)

Multiple Choice:

1. a (1:29; 1:45-49;
      20:24-29; 21:1-19;
      3:1-13; 19:38-42)
2. b (13:15)
3. e (17:9, 20)
4. e (21:6, 9)

Women:

4 (4:10)
1 (2:3)
2 (11:1-2)
5 (8:10)
3 (20:11-18)

Men:

5 (1:17)   9 (13:26)
3 (1:46)   5 (19:34)
4 (3:4)   7 (19:25-27)
2 (1:29, 36)   6 (20:25)
1 (11:44)   8 (21:15-17)

C. TEACHINGS (11)

1. c (17:21)
2. d (12:32)
3. c (16:33)
4. e (1:32; 7:38-39;
      20:22)

Seven Sayings:
1. Bread of life (6:35, 48)
2. Light of world (8:12)
3. Door (10:7, 9)
4. Good shepherd (10:11, 14)
5. Resurrection and life (11:25)
6. Way, truth, and life (14:6)
7. Real vine (15:1, 5)

D. FEATURES (4)

1. e (20:31)
2. c (p. 11)
3. b (p. 11)
4. d (2:13, 7:2, 10:22, 5:9)

UNIT TEST 1 SCORES

Write the number correct for each category on the blank in the # column.
Follow directions for finding the percent (using % chart below or multiplying as indicated) and record percent in % column.

Category	# Correct		% Score	Directions
A. Structure	_____	=	_____	See chart A for 16 items
B. Narratives	_____	=	_____	See chart B for 19 items
C. Teachings	_____	=	_____	See chart C for 11 items
D. Features	_____	=	_____	# correct times 25 = %
Total (A+B+C+D)	_____	=	_____	# correct times 2 = %

To find the percent scores for A, B, and C, circle the # correct for each in
the chart below. The number below your circle is the percent score. Write
it in the % column for each category above.

A.
#	1	2	3	4	5	6	7	8	9	10	11	12	13	14	15	16	#
%	6	13	19	25	31	38	44	50	56	63	69	75	82	88	94	100	%

B.
#	1	2	3	4	5	6	7	8	9	10	11	12	13	14	15	16	17	18	19	#
%	5	10	16	21	26	31	37	42	48	53	58	63	68	74	79	84	90	95	100	%

C.
#	1	2	3	4	5	6	7	8	9	10	11	#
%	9	18	27	36	45	55	64	73	82	91	100	%

Enter your percent scores on the Unit Growth Record below. Subtract pre-test
scores from unit test scores to determine the growth you have achieved by
your study of this unit.

Before you start Unit 2, be sure to look up the references given on the
answer page for any items you have missed.

UNIT 1 GROWTH RECORD

Category	Pre-test	Section 1	Section 2	Unit Test	Growth
A. Structure	%	%	%	%	%
B. Narratives					
C. Teachings		xxxxxxx			
D. Features			xxxxxxx		
Total					

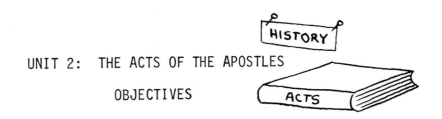

UNIT 2: THE ACTS OF THE APOSTLES

OBJECTIVES

Unit 2 continues the categories used in the Gospels except for the Teachings category. Passages in Acts which contain teachings, such as the sermons and speeches, have been included under Narratives or Features.

After studying Unit 2, you will be able to do the following:

A. In the STRUCTURE category:

    1. State the major structural divisions and subdivisions of Acts.
    2. Place six key events in the order in which they occur in Acts.

B. In the NARRATIVES category:

    1. Associate twelve persons mentioned in Acts with descriptions of them or events in which they took part.
    2. Associate twelve places mentioned in Acts with facts about them or events which occurred there.

C. In the FEATURES category:

    1. Identify a major fact concerning authorship.
    2. Identify the circumstances of writing as presented in this program.
    3. Identify at least two distinguishing features of each of the two major divisions of Acts.
Optional:
    4. Identify the kinds of cultural influences in a particular passage in Acts.
    (This continues the application of a skill learned in Book I, Unit 1.)

As you take the pre-test, you will learn the kinds of information and skills to be mastered in the attainment of these objectives. By comparing your scores before and after doing the guided reading, you will have evidence of the knowledge gained from your study.

Now take the pre-test for Unit 2 beginning on the next page. Remember, you are not expected to do well on any pre-test.

PRE-TEST FOR UNIT 2

A. STRUCTURE

Outline. Circle the letter of the ONE BEST answer for each of the following
statements:

1. The two main divisions of Acts are:
   a. The Missionary Journeys; The Voyage to Rome
   b. Peter and the Church; Paul's Missionary Work
   c. Coming of the Spirit; Building the Church
   d. Birth of the Church; The Church Throughout Palestine
   e. Work of Stephen and Philip; Work of Paul

2. The first major division has the following subdivisions:
   a. The Church in Palestine; The Church in the World
   b. The Apostles; The Helpers
   c. Peter's Work; Philip's Work
   d. The Church in Jerusalem; Extending the Church
   e. Preaching and Healing; Confrontations

3. The second major division has the following subdivisions:
   a. First Journey; Second Journey; Third Journey
   b. Converting the Jews; Missions to the Gentiles
   c. Peter's Work; Paul's Work
   d. Work at Home; Work Abroad
   e. Three Missionary Journeys; Arrest, Trials, Imprisonment

4. Paul's work carried him into ALL of the following areas EXCEPT:
   a. Alexandria
   b. Asia Minor
   c. Macedonia
   d. Greece
   e. Italy

Sequence. Number the following items from 1 to 6 in order of their occurrence
in Acts:

_____Baptism of Cornelius
_____Council freed Peter and John
_____Shipwreck at Malta
_____Three years in Ephesus
_____Ascension
_____Stoning in Antioch of Pisidia

B. NARRATIVES

Places. Write the number of EACH place (right) before the ONE phrase (left)
with which it is most closely associated:

1. _____ Baptism of Gentiles   1. Jerusalem
2. _____ Paul was left for dead   2. Damascus
3. _____ Ridicule of Paul's speech   3. Caesarea   (cont.)

46

Places (continued)

4. ____ Coming of Holy Spirit to Apostles
5. ____ Where Paul was first sent to work
6. ____ Paul's final imprisonment
7. ____ Saul's baptism
8. ____ Philippian jailer baptized
9. ____ Spirit called Barnabas and Paul
10. ____ Paul's 1 1/2-year stay
11. ____ Paul's 3-year stay

4. Antioch of Syria
5. Cyprus
6. Lystra
7. Ephesus
8. Macedonia
9. Corinth
10. Athens
11. Rome

Persons. Write the number of each person's name before the phrase with which it is most closely associated. Use each name ONCE, except those marked "twice."

1. ____ Went first to Jews, then to Gentiles
2. ____ Vision of animals
3. ____ Paul's companion on first mission
4. ____ Knew only baptism of John
5. ____ Stoned to death
6. ____ Helped Paul and Barnabas in Cyprus
7. ____ Carried Jerusalem letter to Antioch
8. ____ Heard Paul's case
9. ____ Baptized an Ethiopian
10. ____ Convert helped in Corinth, Ephesus
11. ____ First baptized Gentile
12. ____ Went back to work after stoning
13. ____ Assistant from Lystra
14. ____ Sermon at Pentecost

1. Philip
2. Peter (twice)
3. Stephen
4. Silas
5. Paul (twice)
6. Barnabas
7. Aquila
8. John Mark
9. Timothy
10. Felix and Festus
11. Cornelius
12. Apollos

C. FEATURES

Background. Circle the letter of the ONE BEST answer:

1. Acts was written as the sequel to (second part of):
    a. The Gospels
    b. Matthew's Gospel
    c. Luke's Gospel
    d. Paul's Letters
    e. Church history

2. When Acts was being written, Christians were:
    a. Expelled from the synagogues
    b. Viewed with suspicion by Rome
    c. Mainly Gentiles
    d. a and c
    e. a, b, and c.

3. The purpose of writing Acts was to:
    a. Describe the expansion of the church
    b. Convert the Jews
    c. Explain the teachings of Jesus
    d. a and b
    e. a, b, and c

Content/Themes

"Firsts." Circle the number of each "first" recorded in Acts.

1. Acceptance of the teachings
   of Jesus
2. Coming of Holy Spirit to the church
3. Christian martyred
4. Apostles chosen
5. Church Council

6. Gentile Christian baptized
7. Jewish Christian baptized
8. Selection of church officers
9. European church
10. Christian creed

"Peter and Paul." Identify the following terms by writing <u>Peter</u> before two terms which are distinctive of his work, and <u>Paul</u> before two terms which are distinctive of Paul's work.

1. _____ Responsible mostly for Jews
2. _____ Responsible mostly for Gentiles
3. _____ Emphasizes life of Jesus
4. _____ Lack of faith

5. _____ Recognition by Rome
6. _____ Training of missionary
           assistants
7. _____ Peaceful ministry
8. _____ Miracles are performed

Circle the ONE BEST answer for each of the following:

The "pattern" of Paul's mission work was to:
   a. Go to the synagogue; then to the Gentiles
   b. Preach; perform miracles; baptize
   c. Convert Roman citizens; win local authorities; be recognized by Rome
   d. Build strong Jewish churches; then mixed churches; then Gentile
      churches
   e. a and d

The "main theme" of Acts is:
   a. An all-inclusive church: Jews and Gentiles
   b. Winning acceptance by Rome
   c. The turn to the Gentiles
   d. Growing division in the early church
   e. Growing unity among the disciples

Check your answers on page 85. Compute your scores there and enter the results on the Unit 2 Growth Record, page 90.

UNIT 2: THE ACTS OF THE APOSTLES

INSTRUCTIONS

The Acts of the Apostles is usually thought of as a history of the primitive church, and it is in fact volume 2 of the two-volume work Luke-Acts. However, another way to approach Acts is to read it as an exciting adventure of dedicated men and women, filled with the Holy Spirit. You will not want to approach Acts this way all the time, but one such reading may well increase your appreciation of these vital people as you gain understanding of the church's story.

So this time, enter into the excitement of the dangers, the political forces, and the victories that these early Christians experienced.

You will not be expected to remember all the names and places in the guided reading questions or even in the charts. However, they will help you to follow and understand the story. The parts you are expected to learn and remember are listed under objectives and demonstrated in the pre-test.

For the rest, move along and enjoy the inspiring story of these energetic and courageous Christians. "Acts" is a most appropriate title.

While the Book of Acts contains two major sections, one dominated by Peter (chs. 1-12) and the other by Paul (chs. 13-28), for the purpose of page layout the content has been divided into three study sections. The major section on Paul has been subdivided into two study sections. The study sections are as follows:

    10's Peter (Acts 1--12)

    20's Paul's first and second journeys (Acts 13--18:23)

    30's Paul's third journey and trip to Rome (Acts 18:24--28)

Use the same study method as in Unit 1, described on page 12.

Structure is taught by "building churches" a level at a time, and Narratives by small maps. Here are the outline structures:

The story you are about to read describes the birth of the church in
Jerusalem and its spread throughout much of the known world. This map
might help you follow the action.

EXTENDING THE CHURCH A.D. 30-60

50

10 BACKGROUND OF ACTS

AUTHOR: Same as Gospel of Luke, anonymous; no name given in text.
            Alternatively, some other Gentile Christian.

DATE: After Gospel of Luke, between A.D. 78 and 100.

READERS: Gentiles. "Theophilus" (1:1) may be an individual or may represent
            any "lover of God" who is a Christian inquirer.

CIRCUM-   There had been more than three decades of unfulfilled hope for the
STANCES: Lord's immediate return in glory. Christians were separated or
            expelled from synagogues, and Gentiles were pouring into the church.
            Christians were viewed with suspicion by Roman authorities.

PURPOSE: To tell how the church in its first 30 years expanded under the power
            and guidance of the Holy Spirit. To rethink history with Jesus
            Christ as midpoint. To justify the mission to Gentiles. To
            defend Christianity against charges of heresy (Jews) and treason
            (Romans).

Go on to the top of the next page.
****

20 PAUL'S MISSIONARY WORK (chs. 13-28)

In these chapters, the author describes the expan-
sion of the church throughout much of the known
world, with Paul as its leader. As Jews rejected the Christian message, Gentiles were
approached. By the end of Acts, the church had
turned to Gentiles as its major source of
members.

21 FIRST JOURNEY (chs. 13-15)

21A Cyprus. READ: Acts 13

1. What did the Holy Spirit command
   the Antioch church to do? (Syria)
   ****

31 THIRD JOURNEY (18:23--21:26)

31A Ephesus. READ: Acts 18:23-28 and ch. 19

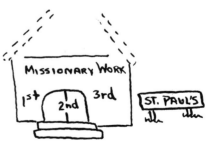

1. Apollos, an outstanding preacher,
   knew only the baptism of John.
   Who corrected him?

10 BACKGROUND

Complete the blanks in #1, and circle the letter of the ONE BEST answer in both 2 and 3.

1. The author of Acts, _____, wrote the book between _____.

2. Readers were:
   a. Jews
   b. Gentiles
   c. Jews and Gentiles
   d. Gentiles in Syria
   e. Jerusalem church

3. Acts was written at a time when ALL of the following were true EXCEPT:
   a. Jesus' expected return did not occur.
   b. Rome took kind view of Christians.
   c. Christians were expelled from synagogues.
   d. Many Gentiles entered church.

Check answers from background information on previous page.

Go on to the top of the next page.

****

21A

1. The Antioch church was told to set apart Barnabas and Saul for the work to which the Spirit had called them.

****

31A

1. Aquila and Priscilla took Apollos aside and taught him correctly.

11 PROLOGUE. READ: Acts 1:1-5

1. Acts is the sequel to which book?
   (See page 49.)

12 PETER AND THE CHURCH (chs. 1-12)

In the first twelve chapters of
Acts, the beginnings of the Christian church are described, with
Peter as the leader of the Christians,
who were almost all Jews.

Go on to the top of the next page.

****

21A Cyprus

2. Who helped Barnabas and Saul
   at Cyprus?

3. What did Governor Sergius Paulus
   do when he saw that Elymas had
   been blinded for his opposition
   to the Christians?
   (Note that verse 9 is the first
   mention of Saul as Paul.)

****

31A

2. Who taught Apollos' disciples about
   the Holy Spirit and baptized them so
   that they received the Holy Spirit?

3. How long did Paul stay in Ephesus?

4. When the seven sons of Sceva were
   attacked by the evil spirits, what
   did the believers do?

5. Who started a riot in Ephesus?

11

1. Luke (Luke-Acts is one work in two parts.)

12

In Matthew 16 Jesus called Peter a rock: "You are a rock, Peter, and on this rock I will build my church."

In Acts Peter witnessed and worked to help Christ build his church.

Continue with 13 on the next page.

****

21A

2. John Mark

3. He believed.

****

31A

2. Paul

3. More than two years (19:8, 10)
   (20:31 says three years)

4. They burned books on magic,
   which they had been using
   secretly.

5. Demetrius, the silversmith

13 THE CHURCH AT JERUSALEM

13A The Birth of the Church. READ: Acts 1--2

1. What happened to Jesus?

2. Lots were drawn in the Upper Room
   to choose a replacement for Judas
   Iscariot. What were the names of
   the twelve apostles then?
   (You might already know the first
   four, the tax collector, and one
   or two from John. Now, who are
   the replacement and the four others?)

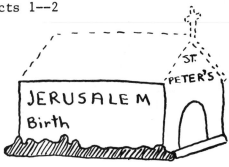

3. The three signs which accompanied the first coming of the Holy Spirit
   to the church led some onlookers to say that the disciples were drunk.
   Who explained to the crowd and gave a sermon that day of Pentecost?

****

21B Asia Minor

1. Who followed Paul and Barnabas out of the synagogue after Paul's
   sermon in the synagogue at Antioch of Pisidia?
   (Note: Paul usually began his missionary work in a new town by
   speaking in a synagogue.)

2. When the jealous Jews insulted Paul, what action did he and
   Barnabas take? (This was the pattern which Paul followed in his
   missionary work.)

3. What did the Jews do to
   Paul and Barnabas then?

****

31B Troas and Miletus. READ: Acts 20

1. When Eutychus died by falling from a window while Paul was preaching in
   Troas, what did Paul do?

2. What did Paul do at Miletus?

13A

1. He was taken up into heaven.
   (the ascension)

2. Peter, James, John, Andrew,
   Matthew, Philip, Thomas,
   Bartholomew, James, Simon,
   Judas, and <u>Matthias</u> (new)

3. Peter gave the sermon, after
   explaining that the disciples
   were fulfilling Joel's prophecy.

****

21B

1. Many Jews and many
   Gentiles who had been
   converted to Judaism

2. Paul and Barnabas left
   the Jews and preached
   to the Gentiles.

3. The Jews threw Paul and
   Barnabas out of the region.

****

31B

1. He hugged him and
   brought him back to life.

2. He said farewell to
   the elders of Ephesus.

13B The First Work of the Church.   READ: Acts 3--5

1. The Jews at the Temple were impressed with Peter and John's healing
   a man at the Beautiful Gate, so Peter then preached to them inside the
   Temple.   What happened to Peter and John?

2. Why did the Council (Sanhedrin)
   set them free?

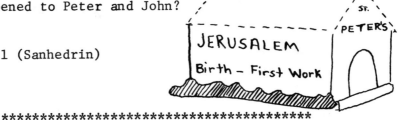

****

21B Asia Minor
   READ: Acts 14--15

4. After a great number of Jews and
   Gentiles were converted by the
   preaching of Paul and Barnabas
   in Iconium, what did some Gentiles
   and Jews plan to do?

5. Who was healed in Lystra?

6. When the Jews from Pisidian Antioch
   influenced the crowds, what did they
   do to Paul?   What did Paul do?

****

31C Caesarea.   READ: Acts 21:1-26

At Caesarea the prophet Agabus
predicted Paul's death.   How
did Paul respond?

31D

1. Where did Paul give a report
   on his work among the Gentiles?

2. Because there were reports that
   Paul was teaching Jews to forsake
   the Law, what ceremony did the
   elders ask Paul to perform?

13B

1. The Sadducees arrested them for teaching that Jesus was raised from death.

2. Because they could not deny the healing of the lame man

****

21B

4. They planned to stone Paul and Barnabas.

5. A crippled man

6. They stoned Paul and dragged him out of town, leaving him for dead.

   Paul got up and went on to Derbe.

****

31C

"I am ready ... to die."

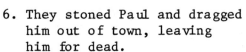

31D

1. Jerusalem

2. The purification ceremony

Turn to page 76 to complete blanks 1-10 on the section chart. Check your answers on page 78, study corrected chart, and then continue work on page 59.

13B First Work

3. What did the believers do with their possessions?

4. After the Sadducees arrested the apostles, they were found teaching
   in the Temple. How did that happen and what did Gamaliel advise the
   Council (Sanhedrin) to do? (Gamaliel had been Paul's teacher. See
   Acts 22:3.)

****

21C The Return

1. What did Paul do in Antioch (of Syria)?

   The Council at Jerusalem was not only
   the first such council, but also
   a turning point for the church. As a
   whole church, they decided that
   Christians did not have to be Jews.

   Note that this meeting is described
   in chapter 15. Judas and Silas took
   a letter from the Jerusalem church
   to the Antioch church.

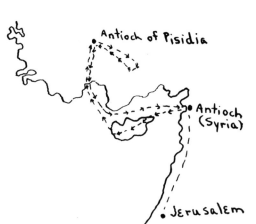

2. What good news did the letter contain?

****

JUST FOR FUN!! Speak to Your Audience

Suppose you were asked to speak about the Christian faith to a group of
businessmen one week and to a group of drug addicts the next. If you
cared anything at all about their response, you know you could not use
the same speech both times! Try to identify the points of difference
which you should consider:

1. What does each group value?
2. What are some major principles on which each group bases its decisions?
3. What sort of background for living--social, educational, recreational--
   does each group have?
4. What patterns of thought does each group tend to use?
5. Is there anything you can say at the beginning to capture their
   confidence? Their interest?

(Continued on bottom section of next page.)

13B

3. They sold them and shared the money to provide a living for the believers.

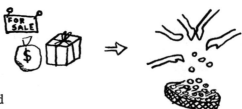

4. An angel freed the apostles and told them to speak in the Temple. Gamaliel advised leaving the apostles alone.

Turn to page 73 to complete blanks 1-9 on the section chart. Check your answers on page 78 and study the corrected chart. Then turn back to continue your work on page 61.

****

21C

1. Paul reported on his work among the Gentiles.

2. Gentiles need not be circumcised in order to become Christians.

NOT NECESSARILY

Now turn to page 74 to complete the section chart on the First Journey. After checking your answers on page 78, study the corrected chart and then continue your work on page 61.

****

JUST FOR FUN!! Speak to Your Audience

Paul faced this problem; so did Peter and most of the disciples. Look up the following sermons and speeches and see if the disciples paid attention to any of the above-mentioned considerations (or to others which may have been more important then) in making their talks to Gentiles different from those to Jews.

To Jews	To Gentiles
Peter: 2:14-36 (Pentecost)	Peter: 10:34-43 (Cornelius)
Paul: 13:16-41 (Antioch of Pisidia)	Paul: 14:15-17 (Lystra)
Paul: 22:1-21 (Defense at fort)	Paul: 17:22-31 (Athens)

JUST FOR FUN!!   Church at Jerusalem Crossword

No Just for Fun is tested; all are just for fun! You need not do any
unless you wish. You may enjoy this puzzle.

Across
1. Man healed at Temple had been _____.
3. Called beautiful
7. She and husband struck dead
8. Not a Gentile
9. What some called the disciples at
   Pentecost
12. What you'll say when you finish this
    puzzle
13. Time when Holy Spirit first came
    to church
15. Disciples _____ possessions
16. What Barnabas sold
17. _____ will be witnesses for me

Down

1. What Peter healed
   in Temple
2. Replaced Judas
4. What Ananias became
   after deception
5. Group which freed
   Peter and John

6. Pharisees kept this
7. What beggar took each day at Temple
10. What the apostles said Jesus was
11. Preached sermon at Pentecost
12. First part of name: filled disciples
14. What the apostles did to new converts
16. Tongues of _____

****

JUST FOR FUN!!   An Appropriate Pattern

   Paul's pattern in missionary work was to speak in the synagogue first.
Usually the Jews insulted or attacked him, so he left to preach to the
Gentiles. What might have been the results if Paul had gone first to
the Gentiles? Why do you think he found it worth the attacks, the risk
of death?

   More related to this on the next page ...

****

32 ARREST, TRIALS, AND IMPRISONMENT (21:27--28:22)

32A The Arrest. READ: Acts 21:27-40 and chs. 22-23

What happened when the Jews saw Paul
in the Temple at Jerusalem?

JUST FOR FUN!!   Church at Jerusalem Crossword

Answers:

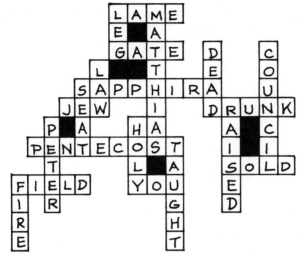

****

JUST FOR FUN!!   An Appropriate Pattern

Can you think of any parallels today?

Is there any pattern which a Christian would be wise to consider in his dealings with such groups as the following:

1. Intellectual agnostics
2. Hippies
3. Old "diehards"
4. Young "revolutionaries"
5. Sophisticated socialites
6. Members of church groups very different from one's own
7. Members of one's own church group

Do any of the above suggest parallel groups in the New Testament?

****

32A

1. They dragged him out of the Temple and beat him. The Roman commander stopped the commotion by arresting Paul.

62

14 EXTENDING THE CHURCH (chs. 6-12)

14A Stephen's Work. READ: Acts 6--7

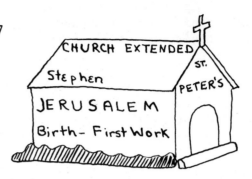

1. Which group was being neglected when seven helpers were chosen?

2. Some Jews paid men to lie about Stephen so they could arrest him. Why did Stephen's speech anger the Council (Sanhedrin)?

3. How did Stephen die? Who approved?

****

22 SECOND JOURNEY (16:1--18:22)

22A Asia Minor. READ: Acts 16

After Paul and Silas arrived in Lystra, Paul chose a new assistant who helped Paul and Silas deliver the Jerusalem decision to the surrounding towns. Who was he?

22B Macedonia

1. Why did Paul go to Macedonia?

****

32A The Arrest

2. Where did Paul make a speech of defense? What saved him from a whipping?

3. How did Paul divide the Council (Sanhedrin) concerning him?

14A

1. Greek-speaking Jewish Christians. They said their widows were not receiving their share of the funds.

2. Stephen said the Council members did not obey the Law.

3. He was stoned to death.

   Saul approved.

****

22A

Timothy

22B

1. He was told in a vision to go.

****

32A

2. At the fort

   His Roman citizenship

3. By saying he had been arrested because he believed in the resurrection, and so setting Pharisees against Saducees

14B Philip's Work. READ: Acts 8

1. After Stephen's death, the
   Christians were attacked by
   the Jews so that they had to
   scatter throughout Palestine,
   Syria, Cyprus, etc. Where
   did Philip (one of the seven
   helpers) preach?

2. Who was baptized by Philip on
   the road to Gaza?

****

22B Macedonia

2. After baptizing Lydia, Paul
   and Silas drove a demon out
   of a slave girl and were
   put in prison. Why?

3. Who believed after an earthquake freed Paul and Silas
   from the jail?

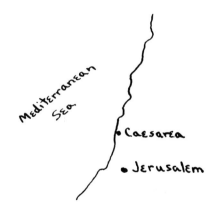

****

32B The Trials. READ: Acts 24--26

1. The High Priest, some elders,
   and a lawyer accused Paul
   before what official?
   Where?

2. When Festus became governor,
   the Jews planned again to
   kill Paul. Knowing this,
   what did Paul do?

3. The story of Paul's conversion
   appears a third time in his defense
   before what official?

14B

1. Philip preached in Samaria.
After leaving the road to
Gaza he preached in Judea
on his way back to Caesarea.

2. The Ethiopian official

****

22B

2. Because she could no
longer earn money for
her masters with her
prophecies

3. The jailer in Philippi

****

32B

1. Before the Roman governor
Felix in Caesarea

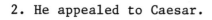

2. He appealed to Caesar.

3. King Agrippa, on an official visit to Festus

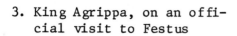

14C Saul's Work. READ: Acts 9:1-31

1. Why did Saul ask for letters of introduction to the Damascus synagogues?

2. Who stopped Saul on the way?

****

22B Macedonia. READ: Acts 17:1-15

4. In Thessalonica the jealous Jews formed a mob looking for Paul and Silas. When night came, what did Paul and Silas do?

5. Many people of Berea were converted, so Jews from Thessalonica stirred up mobs to attack Paul and Silas. What did the disciples do for Paul then?

****

32C To Rome as Prisoner. READ: Acts 27

1. Paul was sent to Rome by ship. When bad weather came, where did they hope to spend the winter?

2. Paul had predicted a shipwreck. During the bad storm, the sailors tried to abandon ship. Who insisted that they be stopped?

3. At the time of the shipwreck, what did the soldiers plan to do?

14C

1. So he could arrest any believers he found there and take them back to Jerusalem.

2. Saul saw a blinding light and heard Jesus speaking to him.

****

22B

4. They left for Berea in the night.

5. Sent Paul away and went with him as far as Athens

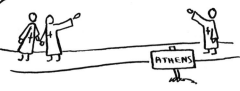

****

32C

1. In a harbor (Phoenix) in Crete

2. Paul spoke to the army officer and the soldiers, who cut the ropes on the boat.

3. They planned to kill the prisoners.

14D Peter's Work. READ: Acts 9:32-43 and ch. 10

1. What did Peter do for Dorcas of Joppa?

2. What was Peter warned about in his
   vision of animals?

3. As a result of his vision, Peter
   went to a Gentile's house. He
   explained why he was acting con-
   trary to the Jewish Law. Then
   what did he see happening to these
   Gentiles? So what did Peter order?

****

22C Greece. READ: Acts 17:16--18:22

1. In Athens some Epicurean and Stoic
   teachers asked Paul to speak to the
   Areopagus (Council). What did they
   think of Paul's speech?

2. In Corinth what Jewish tentmaker
   and his Roman wife helped Paul?

3. When the Jews opposed Paul in
   Corinth, he followed his usual pattern.
   What was this?

****

32C To Rome as Prisoner

4. Who escaped alive from the
   shipwreck at Malta?

   READ: Acts 28:1-22

5. How did Paul live in Rome?

14D

1. He brought her
   back to life.

2. Not to call unclean
   what God calls clean

3. They received the Holy
   Spirit. Then Peter
   ordered that they be
   baptized. (Note: First
   baptism of Gentiles.)

****

22C

1. They made fun of Paul.

2. Aquila and Priscilla

3. First he went to the
   synagogue. When Jews
   rejected him, he would
   go to the Gentiles.

****

32C

4. All escaped.

5. He was allowed to live
   alone in his house
   under guard.

14D Peter's Work. READ: Acts 11--12

4. It was hard for the Jewish Christians to accept Gentiles. When
   the Jerusalem Christians criticized Peter for his work in Caesarea,
   what did he do to change their minds?

5. Next, Jerusalem Christians heard that Christians in Antioch were
   preaching to the Gentiles. What did the Jerusalem church do?

6. What new name were the disciples given in Antioch?

7. How did Peter escape after Herod imprisoned him?

****

22C Greece

4. In a vision Paul was reassured about his safety. How long
   did Paul stay in Corinth?

5. When the Jews took Paul to court, what did the Roman
   governor do?

****

33 CONCLUSION: TURN TO THE GENTILES COMPLETED
   READ: Acts 28:23-31

In Rome the Jews came to hear Paul.

1. When many would not believe,
   whom did Paul quote?

2. To whom did Paul say God's
   message had been sent?

14D

4. He told them of the vision
   and of the coming of the
   Holy Spirit to the Gentiles.

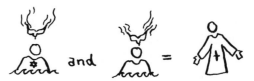

5. It sent Barnabas to investigate.

6. Christians

7. An angel freed him.

Turn to page 73 and complete blanks 10-20 on the section chart. Check your answers on page 78. After studying corrected chart, turn to page 79 and take Section Test 1.

****

22C

4. One and a half years

5. Drove the Jews out of court

Now turn to page 75 to complete blanks 1-10 on the section chart of the Second Journey. Check your answers on page 78 and study the corrected chart. Then turn to page 81 and take Section Test 2.

****

33

1. Isaiah

2. To the Gentiles

Turn to page 77 to complete blanks 1-10 on the section chart. After checking your answers on page 78, study the corrected chart. Then turn to page 83 and take Section Test 3.

72

You may want to write the answers on a separate sheet first. If necessary, look up the remaining answers. Then write the answers in the blanks from memory.

Christians of
(1) _____
Faith

Preaching in
Palestine

_____

THE CHURCH AT JERUSALEM Chs. 1-5

_____

(2) _____of Jesus

Election of Matthias

(3) Coming of _____

(4) Sermon by
_____

(5) Healing _____

Peter's message at Temple

Victory of (6) _____
and (7) _____
over Council

(8) _____all
possessions

Miracles

Victory of (9) _____
over Council

_____

EXTENDING THE CHURCH Chs. 6-12

(10) _____Helpers
    (number)

Miracles

Speech to Council

Death by
(11) _____

Preached in
(12) _____

Baptized the
official from
(13) _____

(14) _____
    Christians

(15) _____
on road to
Damascus

Raising (16) _____
in Joppa

Seeing Gentiles (17) ___
_____

(18) _____the Gentiles

Report to (19) _____
_____

Sending Barnabas to
Antioch

Escape from
(20) _____

Check answers on page 78. Correct them, then study chart.

SECTION CHART 2A: ACTS

Study the following chart and complete the blanks from memory, following instructions given for Section Chart 1.

Converts were mainly

(1) _____

Preached to much of known world

FIRST JOURNEY Chs. 13-15

Barnabas and (2) _____ were sent on mission

ANTIOCH

S y r i a

John Mark helped

Magician opposed

Magician was (3) _____

Governor believed

CYPRUS

M e d i t e r r a n e a n

Sermon

Insults ⟹

Preached to (4) _____

Gentile believers

PISIDIAN ANTIOCH

A s i a   M i n o r

Preached ⟹ Conversions

Plots to (5) _____ the apostles ⟹ Preached elsewhere

ICONIUM

A s i a   M i n o r

The Jews

(6) _____ Paul

⟹ Paul got up and went on

LYSTRA

A s i a   M i n o r

Paul gave report on

(7) _____

(8) _____

S y r i a

COUNCIL

(9) Acts chapter ____

J e r u s a l e m

Paul and Silas went to Antioch

To Church at Antioch:

NO

(10) _____

for Gentiles

Check answers on p. 78. Study corrected chart, then continue on p. 61.

Study the following chart and complete the blanks from memory, following instructions given for Section Chart 1.

SECOND JOURNEY 16:1--18:22

Chose (1) _____

Delivered rules from

(2) _____

[LYSTRA]

A s i a   M i n o r

Paul's

(3) _____ Went to Macedonia

[TROAS]

A s i a   M i n o r

Talked to ⟶ Baptized
women   (4) _____

Drove out   (5) _____
demons   freed them

Paul and Silas   Jailer
jailed   believed

[PHILIPPI]

M a c e d o n i a

Preached
(6) _____ went

after Paul ⟶ Paul and
and Silas   Silas left

[THESSALONICA]

M a c e d o n i a

Preached ⟶ Many
                 (7) _____

Mobs ⟶ Paul left for
           Athens

[BEREA]

M a c e d o n i a

Speech to ⟶ A few
Areopagus   believers

Greeks   Paul went
(8) _____   on
_____

[ATHENS]

G r e e c e

Lived with
Aquila

Evil sayings ⟶

Left Jews for
Gentiles

Synagogue
leader
believed

[CORINTH 1½ years]

G r e e c e

Vision of
protection

(9) _____ taken   Roman
to court ⟶ governor
             (10) _____
             _____

Check answers on p. 78. Study charts 2A and 2B, then take Sect. Test 2, p. 81.

PAUL'S THIRD JOURNEY   18:23--21:26

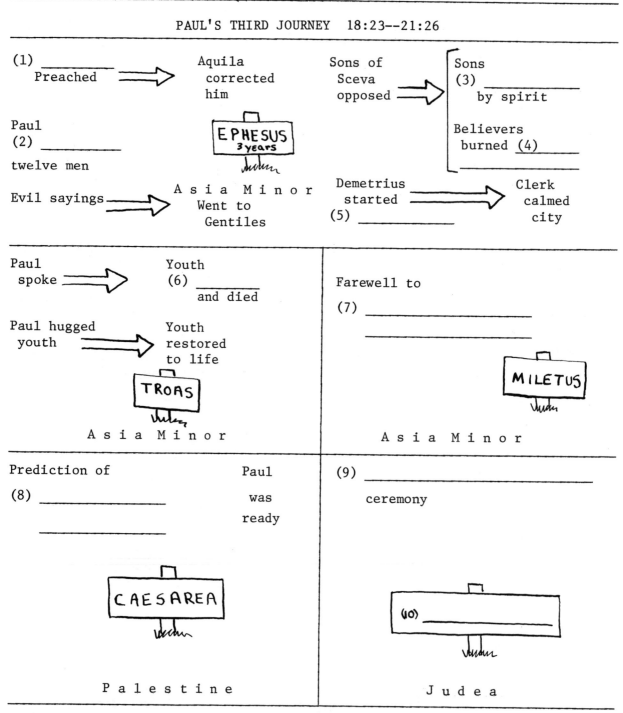

(1) _____
        Preached ⟶ Aquila
                    corrected
                    him

Sons of
Sceva ⟶ Sons
opposed   (3) _____
                    by spirit

Paul
(2) _____

twelve men

EPHESUS
3 years

Believers
burned (4) _____

Evil sayings ⟶ A s i a   M i n o r
                Went to
                Gentiles

Demetrius
started ⟶ Clerk
(5) _____   calmed
                    city

Paul
spoke ⟶ Youth
        (6) _____
            and died

Farewell to
(7) _____
_____

Paul hugged
youth ⟶ Youth
        restored
        to life

TROAS

MILETUS

A s i a   M i n o r

A s i a   M i n o r

Prediction of
(8) _____
_____

Paul
was
ready

(9) _____

ceremony

CAESAREA

(10) _____

P a l e s t i n e

J u d e a

Check answers on page 78. Study corrected chart, then turn to the bottom of
page 59 to continue your work.

76

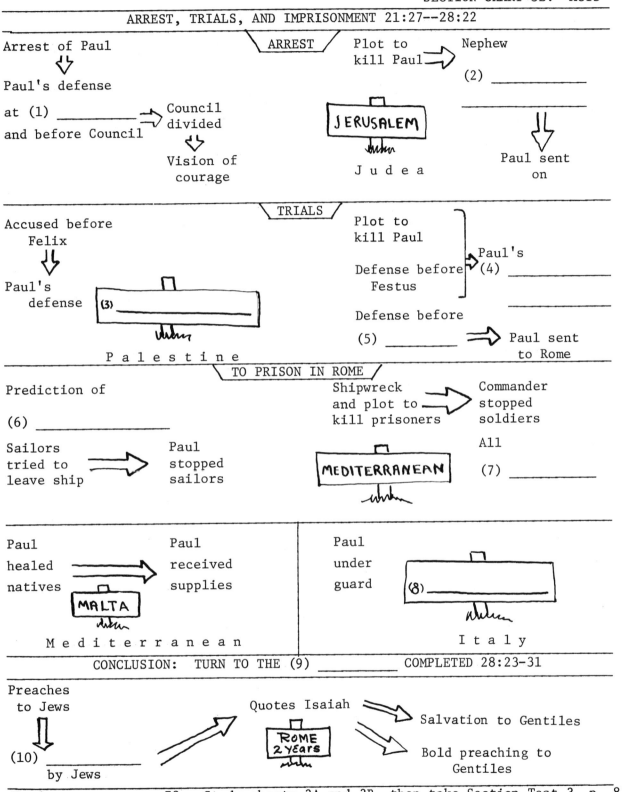

ARREST, TRIALS, AND IMPRISONMENT 21:27--28:22

Arrest of Paul ⟍ARREST⟋ Plot to kill Paul ⟹ Nephew

(2) _____

Paul's defense

at (1) _____ ⟹ Council divided
and before Council

JERUSALEM

Judea

Vision of courage

Paul sent on

⟍TRIALS⟋

Accused before Felix

Plot to kill Paul

Defense before Festus ⟍ Paul's (4) _____

Paul's defense (3) _____

_____

Defense before (5) _____ ⟹ Paul sent to Rome

Palestine

⟍TO PRISON IN ROME⟋

Prediction of (6) _____

Shipwreck and plot to kill prisoners ⟹ Commander stopped soldiers

Sailors tried to leave ship ⟹ Paul stopped sailors

MEDITERRANEAN

All (7) _____

Paul healed natives ⟹ Paul received supplies

MALTA

Mediterranean

Paul under guard

(8) _____

Italy

CONCLUSION: TURN TO THE (9) _____ COMPLETED 28:23-31

Preaches to Jews

(10) _____
by Jews

Quotes Isaiah ⟹ Salvation to Gentiles

ROME 2 Years

⟹ Bold preaching to Gentiles

Check answers on p. 78. Study charts 3A and 3B, then take Section Test 3, p. 83.

ANSWERS TO SECTION CHARTS

Section Chart 1

Church at Jerusalem

1. Jewish
2. Ascension
3. Holy Spirit
4. Peter
5. Lame man
6. Peter
7. John
8. Sharing
9. Apostles

Extending the Church

10. Seven
11. Stoning
12. Samaria
13. Ethiopia
14. Persecuted
15. Converted
16. Dorcas
17. Receive the Holy Spirit
18. Baptizing
19. Jerusalem church
20. Prison

Section Chart 2

A. First Journey

1. Gentiles
2. Saul
3. Blinded
4. Gentiles
5. Stone (kill)
6. Stoned
7. Mission to the Gentiles
8. Antioch
9. 15
10. Circumcision

B. Second Journey

1. Timothy
2. Jerusalem
3. Vision
4. Lydia
5. Earthquake
6. Mob
7. Converted
8. Made fun of Paul
9. Paul
10. Drove Jews out of court

Section Chart 3

A. Third Journey

1. Apollos
2. Baptized
3. Attacked
4. Books of magic
5. Riot
6. Fell
7. Ephesus elders
8. Paul's death
9. Purification
10. Jerusalem

B. Arrest, Trials, Imprisonment

1. Fort
2. Warned commander
3. Caesarea
4. Appeal to Emperor
5. Agrippa
6. Shipwreck
7. Safe
8. Rome
9. Gentiles
10. Rejection

SECTION TEST 1

A. STRUCTURE

Outline. Fill in the blanks to complete the following outline:

PETER AND THE CHURCH

I. The Church at (1) _____

    A. The (2) _____ of the Church

    B. The (3) _____ of the Church

II. (4) _____ the Church

    A. (5) _____

    B. (6) _____

    C. (7) _____

    D. (8) _____

Sequence. Number the items in each group from 1 to 6 in order of their occurrence in Acts:

In Jerusalem	Beyond Jerusalem
____ Peter's Pentecost sermon	____ Peter imprisoned by Herod
____ Ascension	____ Barnabas sent to Antioch
____ Coming of the Holy Spirit	____ Stephen stoned to death
____ Apostles led from prison	____ Saul's conversion
____ Ananias and Sapphira die	____ Peter's vision of animals
____ Lame man healed	____ Ethiopian baptized

B. NARRATIVES

Places. Identify the place where each of the following occurred by writing the number of the place before the correct phrase:

____ Baptism of Ethiopian	1. Beautiful Gate
____ Baptism of Cornelius	2. Road to Gaza
____ Disciples called Christians	3. Road to Damascus
____ Conversion of Saul	4. Caesarea
____ Lame man healed	5. Antioch

<u>Persons</u>. Identify the following persons by writing the number of the person (right) on the blank before the term (left) with which the person is most closely associated. Use each name ONCE UNLESS marked twice.

1. _____ One of the seven helpers chosen
2. _____ Stoned by Jews at Jerusalem
3. _____ Baptized Cornelius, the Gentile
4. _____ Advised Council to leave apostles alone
5. _____ Persecuted Christians
6. _____ Approved Stephen's death
7. _____ Investigated Antioch church
8. _____ Chosen by lot to replace Judas
9. _____ Killed James
10. _____ Raised from death
11. _____ Speech angered Council
12. _____ With Paul at Antioch
13. _____ Sermon on Solomon's Porch
14. _____ Baptized Ethiopian
15. _____ Walked for first time

1. Herod
2. Stephen (twice)
3. Man at Temple gate
4. Barnabas (twice)
5. Peter (twice)
6. Dorcas
7. Saul (twice)
8. Philip (twice)
9. Matthias
10. Gamaliel

C. FEATURES

Circle the numbers of ten phrases which are distinctive features of the church in this section, Peter and the Church, Acts 1--12:

1. Most Christians in Palestine
2. First written document
3. First called Christians
4. First predominantly Gentile church
5. Most converts Gentiles
6. Most converts Jews
7. First church persecution
8. Accepted by Jewish leaders
9. Missionary work in Asia Minor
10. First selection of officers
11. First Christian martyr
12. Paul was leader
13. Miracles performed
14. First baptism of a Gentile
15. Peter was leader
16. Established congregations
17. Most Christians outside Palestine
18. Turn to the Gentiles completed

Check your answers on page 86 and compute your scores below.

SECTION TEST 1 SCORES

Category	# Correct	% Score	Directions
A. Structure	_____ = _____		# Correct times 5 = %
B. Narratives	_____ = _____		# Correct times 5 = %
C. Features	_____ = _____		# Correct times 10 = %
Total (A+B+C)	_____ = _____		# Correct times 2 = %

Enter your percent scores on the Growth Record on page 90. Review the material for any items you missed. Then turn to page 51 to begin the study of Section 2.

SECTION TEST 2

A. STRUCTURE

Outline. Fill in the blanks to complete the following outline of the
first half of Paul's missionary work:

PAUL'S MISSIONARY WORK

I. The (1) _____

   A. (2) _____

   B. Asia Minor

      1. (3) _____ of Pisidia
      2. Iconium
      3. Lystra and Derbe

   C. The Return
      1. Antioch Report
      2. (4) _____ Ch. 15

II. The (5) _____

   A. (6) _____ : Timothy

   B. (7) _____
      1. Philippi: Lydia and Jailer
      2. Thessalonian Mob
      3. Berea: Converts and Mob

   C. (8) _____
      1. Athens: Ridicule
      2. Corinth: Aquila and Priscilla

Sequence. Number the items in each of the following groups from 1-6 in order
of their occurrence in the first two journeys in Acts.

First Missionary Journey

____ Paul's sermon in Antioch of
     Pisidia
____ Paul stoned and left for dead
____ Jerusalem Council
____ Holy Spirit called Barnabas
     and Saul
____ Report to Antioch church in
     Syria
____ Barnabas, Saul, and John
     Mark in Cyprus

Second Missionary Journey

____ Lydia baptized
____ Paul speaks in Athens
____ Jailer baptized
____ Roman governor drove
     Jews out of court
____ Aquila helped Paul
____ Timothy helped deliver
     Jerusalem decision

B. NARRATIVES

Places. Write the number of EACH place on the blank before the ONE phrase
with which it is most closely associated.

_____ Mobs looked for Paul and Silas	1.	Jerusalem
_____ Greeks in Berea believed	2.	Athens
_____ Earthquake freed Paul and Silas	3.	Thessalonica
_____ Paul stayed 1½ years	4.	Corinth
_____ Paul spoke to Greek Council	5.	Philippi
_____ First reference to Saul as Paul	6.	Cyprus
_____ First church council	7.	Macedonia

Persons. Write the number of EACH person on the blank before the ONE term
with which the person is most closely associated.

_____ In Philippian jail with Paul	1.	Saul/Paul
_____ Converted Paulus, governor of Cyprus	2.	John Mark
_____ Assistant from Lystra	3.	Timothy
_____ Tentmaker helper in Corinth	4.	Silas
_____ Wife of Aquila; church worker	5.	Aquila
_____ Helped in Cyprus	6.	Priscilla

Check answers on page 86 and compute your scores below.

SECTION TEST 2 SCORES

Category	# Correct		% Score	Directions
A. Structure	_____	=	_____	# Correct times 5 = %
B. Narratives	_____	=	_____	See chart below

Total Score: # correct (A+B) = _____
Multiply by 3   X   3
Add 1   _____ + 1 _____%

#1	2	3	4	5	6	7	8	9	10	11	12	13 #
%8	15	23	31	38	46	54	62	69	77	85	92	100 %

Enter percent scores on Growth Record, page 90. Review the material for any
items you missed. Then turn to page 51 to begin the study of Section 3.

SECTION TEST 3

A. STRUCTURE

Outline. Fill in the blanks to complete the following outline which con-
cludes Paul's missionary work, and the Acts of the Apostles:

PAUL'S MISSIONARY WORK

III. The (1) _____

    A. (2) _____
    B. Troas and Miletus
    C. Caesarea
    D. (3) _____

IV. The (4) _____, _____, and _____

    A. Arrest at the Temple

    B. (5) _____ and Imprisonment
      1. Felix
      2. Festus
      3. Agrippa

    C. Voyage to (6) _____

Sequence. Number the events in each of the following groups from 1 to 5 in
order of their occurrence in this last portion of Acts:

____ Agabus predicts Paul's death   ____ Shipwreck on Malta
____ Eutychus falls out of window   ____ Arrest at Temple
____ Aquila teaches Apollos   ____ Appeal to Caesar
____ Riot started by Demetrius   ____ Plot to kill Paul
____ Farewell to elders   ____ Defense at fort

B. NARRATIVES

Persons. Write the number of EACH person on the blank before the ONE term
with which it is most closely associated.

____ Governor kept Paul imprisoned   1. Paul
     for two years   2. Paul's nephew
____ New governor who heard appeal   3. Agrippa
____ Instructed by Priscilla and Aquila 4. Festus
____ After punishment of these men,   5. Apollos
     Christians burned books of magic 6. Demetrius
____ Divided Council by resurrection   7. Felix
     statement   8. Sons of Sceva
____ King who heard Paul's case
____ Silversmith in Ephesus
____ Revealed plot to kill Paul

Places. Write the number of EACH place on the blank before the ONE term with which it is most closely associated.

_____ Defense at fort	1.	Jerusalem
_____ A stay of three years	2.	Rome
_____ Shipwreck	3.	Caesarea
_____ Final imprisonment	4.	Malta
_____ Paul imprisoned two years	5.	Ephesus

C. FEATURES

Circle the four numbers of features characteristic of the church under Paul's leadership:

1. Most Christians in Judea and Galilee
2. The turn to Gentiles completed
3. Most Christians Gentiles
4. Miracles performed
5. Most Christians outside Palestine
6. First Christian martyr
7. Jews approached first: rejection; then Gentiles: acceptance
8. First predominantly Gentile church

Check your answers on page 86 and compute your scores below.

SECTION TEST 3 SCORES

Category	# Correct	% Score	Directions
A. Structure	_____	= _____	See Chart A below.
B. Narratives	_____	= _____	See Chart B below.
C. Features	_____	= _____	# Correct times 25 = %

Total Score: # Correct (A+B+C) = _____
Multiply by 3   X 3
Add 1   _____ + 1 = _____%

A. #	1	2	3	4	5	6	7	8	9	10	11	12	13	14	15	16	#
%	6	13	19	25	31	38	44	50	56	63	69	75	82	88	94	100	%

B. #	1	2	3	4	5	6	7	8	9	10	11	12	13	#
%	8	15	23	31	38	46	54	62	69	77	85	92	100	%

Enter your percent scores on Growth Record, page 90. Review the material for any items you missed. Then begin Unit Test 2 on page 87.

ANSWERS TO PRE-TEST FOR UNIT 2

A. STRUCTURE (10 questions)   **B. NARRATIVES (25 questions)**

Outline (4)	Sequence (6)		Places (11)			Persons (14)		
1. b	3		1. 3	7. 2		1. 5	8. 10	
2. d	2		2. 6	8. 8		2. 2	9. 1	
3. e	6		3. 10	9. 4		3. 6	10. 7	
4. a	5		4. 1	10. 9		4. 12	11. 11	
	1		5. 5	11. 7		5. 3	12. 5	
	4		6. 11			6. 8	13. 9	
						7. 4	14. 2	

C. FEATURES (15 questions)

Background (3)	Content/Theme (12)						
1. c	Firsts		Peter/Paul		Pattern	Main Theme
2. e	2	6	1	2	a	c
3. a	3	8	8	6		
	5	9				

Compute your scores on the chart below.

Category	# Correct		% Score	Directions
A. Structure	____	=	____	# Correct times 10 = %
B. Narratives	____	=	____	# Correct times 4 = %
C. Features	____	=	____	See Chart C below
Total (A+B+C)	____	=	____	# Correct times 2 = %

To compute Features score, find # correct on chart. Below this number is
the correct percent.

C.	#	1	2	3	4	5	6	7	8	9	10	11	12	13	14	15	#
	%	7	13	20	27	33	40	47	53	60	67	73	80	87	93	100	%

Enter your percent scores on the Growth Record, page 90. Then begin your
study of Unit 2 on page 49.

ANSWERS TO SECTION TESTS IN UNIT 2

Section Test 1

STRUCTURE (20 questions)				NARRATIVES (20 questions)				FEATURES (10)

STRUCTURE (20 questions)

Outline (8)	Sequence (12)	
1. Jerusalem		
2. Birth	3	6
3. First Work	1	5
4. Extending	2	1
5. Stephen	6	3
6. Philip	5	4
7. Saul	4	2
8. Peter		

NARRATIVES (20 questions)

Places (5)	Persons (15)	
2	1. 8	9. 1
4	2. 2	10. 6
5	3. 5	11. 2
3	4. 10	12. 4
1	5. 7	13. 5
	6. 7	14. 8
	7. 4	15. 3
	8. 9	

FEATURES (10)

1
3
4
6
7
10
11
13
14
15

Section Test 2

STRUCTURE (20 questions)

Outline (8)	Sequence (12)	
1. First Missionary	3	2
Journey	4	4
2. Cyprus	6	3
3. Antioch	1	6
4. Jerusalem Council	5	5
5. Second Missionary	2	1
Journey		
6. Asia Minor (Lystra)		
7. Macedonia		
8. Greece		

NARRATIVES (13 questions)

Places (7)	Persons (6)
3	4
7	1
5	3
4	5
2	6
6	2
1	

Section Test 3

STRUCTURE (16 questions)

Outline (6)	Sequence (10)	
1. Third Missionary	5	5
Journey	3	1
2. Ephesus	1	4
3. Jerusalem	2	3
4. Arrest, Trials,	4	2
and Imprisonment		
5. Trials		
6. Rome		

NARRATIVES (13 questions)

Persons (8)	Places (5)
7	1
4	5
5	4
8	2
1	3
3	
6	
2	

FEATURES (4)

2	5
3	7

UNIT TEST 2

A. STRUCTURE

Outline. Fill in the blanks of the following outline of Acts.

   Prologue

I. (1) _____ and the Church

   A. The Church in (2) _____

      1. (3) _____ of the Church

      2. (4) _____ of the Church

   B. (5) _____ the Church

II. (6) _____ Work

   A. First Journey (Cyprus and Asia Minor)
   B. Second Journey (Asia Minor and Europe)
   C. Third Journey (Asia Minor and Samaria)
   D. (7) _____

      1. Arrest in Jerusalem
      2. Felix, Festus, Agrippa in Caesarea
      3. Voyage to (8) _____

   Conclusion: Turn to (9) _____

Sequence. Number the following events in order of their occurrence in Acts.

_____ Stephen's martyrdom
_____ Paul sent to imprisonment in Rome
_____ Peter's Pentecost sermon
_____ Jerusalem church Council
_____ Missionary work in Asia Minor
_____ Victories of apostles over Jewish Council

B. NARRATIVES

Persons. Identify the following persons by writing the number of each person's
name on the blank before the term with which it is most closely associated.
Use each name ONCE UNLESS marked twice.

_____ Jailed at Philippi with Paul   1. Peter (twice)
_____ First to be stoned to death   2. Stephen (twice)
_____ A persecutor converted   3. Philip
_____ Uninformed preacher   4. Saul/Paul (twice)
_____ Heard Paul's case   5. Barnabas
_____ Sermon after coming of Spirit   6. John Mark   (cont.)

Persons (continued)

____ Sent to investigate Antioch church	7. Timothy
____ Cyprus with Barnabas and Saul	8. Aquila and Priscilla
____ Helped Paul in Corinth and Ephesus	9. Silas
____ First Gentile Christian	10. Felix and Festus
____ Said Council members did not obey Law	11. Apollos
____ Defense at fort	12. Cornelius
____ Helped Paul and Silas tell Council decision in Asia Minor	
____ Baptized Ethiopian official	
____ Healed lame man	

Places. Identify the following places by writing the number of each place on the blank before the correct description or event.

____ First church council	1. Athens
____ Predominantly Gentile church	2. Damascus
____ Imprisonment after shipwreck	3. Caesarea
____ The Council made fun of Paul.	4. Antioch of Syria
____ Paul stayed here 1½ years.	5. Cyprus
____ Baptism of Cornelius	6. Asia Minor
____ First stop on first missionary journey	7. Jerusalem
____ Paul stayed here 3 years.	8. Corinth
____ Location of Lystra and Ephesus	9. Ephesus
____ Saul's baptism	10. Rome

C. FEATURES

Background. Circle the ONE BEST answer:

1. Acts was written by:
   a. Paul
   b. Peter
   c. Author of John's Gospel
   d. Author of Luke's Gospel
   e. Author of Matthew's Gospel

2. At the time Acts was written ALL of the following were true of Christians EXCEPT:
   a. They were mainly Gentiles.
   b. They had been expelled from the synagogues.
   c. They were divided by heresies.
   d. They were viewed with suspicion by Roman authorities.
   e. They found that Christ had not returned as soon as some expected.

88

Content/Themes. Circle the TWO correct features in EACH group.

1. Peter's work:
    a. Mainly in Palestine
    b. In Palestine and Asia Minor
    c. In Jerusalem only
    d. Mostly Jewish converts
    e. Mostly Gentile converts

2. Paul's work:
    a. Mainly in Palestine and Europe
    b. Training of assistants
    c. Mostly Jewish converts
    d. To Jews first, then to Gentiles

Cultural Influence. Read Acts 21:37-40 and 22:25, then give the kinds of cultural influence as indicated:

Jewish: (1) _____

Greek: (2) _____

Roman: (3) _____

         (4) _____

If you have not studied Book I of this series, instead of Cultural Influence you may substitute the following.

Circle the letter before each of FOUR distinctive features of the Book of Acts:

    a. Story of what the twelve apostles did
    b. Part of a two-volume work
    c. Holy Spirit plays a prominent role
    d. Tells of the death of Paul
    e. First church history book
    f. Contains 30 chapters
    g. Begins with the ascension of Jesus

Check answers on page 90 and compute your scores on the chart below.
Remember to look up the references for any items you missed.

UNIT 2 SCORES

Category	# Correct	% Score	Directions
A. Structure	____ = ____		See chart below
B. Narratives	____ = ____		# Correct times 4 = %
C. Features	____ = ____		# Correct times 10 = %
Total (A+B+C)	____ = ____		# Correct times 2 = %

A. #	1	2	3	4	5	6	7	8	9	10	11	12	13	14	15	#
%	7	13	20	27	33	40	47	53	60	67	73	80	87	93	100	%

Enter your scores on the Growth Record. p. 90, and calculate your achievement in this study of Acts.

ANSWERS TO UNIT TEST 2

A. STRUCTURE (15 questions)   B. NARRATIVES (25 questions)

Outline (9) See pp. 73-77. Sequence (6)   Persons (15)   Places (10)
1. Peter   3 (7:60)   9 (16:22)   7 (15)
2. Jerusalem   6 (27:1)   2 (7:59)   4 (11:20)
3. The Birth   1 (2:14)   4 (9:3)   10 (28:16)
4. The First Work   5 (15)   11 (18:24-25)   1 (17:32)
5. Extending   4 (13:13)   10 (24:10; 25:22)   8 (18:11)
6. Paul's Missionary   2 (5:17)   1 (2:14)   3 (10:48)
7. Arrest, Trials, and   5 (11:22)   5 (13:4)
     Imprisonment   6 (13:5)   9 (20:31)
8. Rome   8 (18:2, 26)   6 (p. 57 and
9. Gentiles Completed   12 (10)   map p. 50)
                                        2 (7)   2 (9:3)
                                        4 (21:37)
                                        7 (16:3-4)
                                        3 (8:38)
                                        1 (3:6)

C. FEATURES (10 questions)

Background (2)   Cultural Influences (4) or Distinctive Features (4)

   1. d (p. 51)   1. Language, 21:40   b (p. 49)
   2. c (p. 51)   (or man, 21:39)   c (p. 49 and
                              2. Language, 21:37   throughout)
Content/Themes (4)   3. Military occupation   e (p. 49)
   1. a, d (pp. 53, 73)   (commander, fort, soldiers) g (1:9)
   2. b, d (pp. 53, 63;   4. Law, 22:25
              51, 55)   (appeal based on
                                citizenship)

After you have entered all scores in the growth record as instructed, subtract your pre-test score from your unit test score in each category to see
your growth in knowledge of the Acts of the Apostles.

UNIT 2 GROWTH RECORD

Category	Pre-test	Sect. 1	Sect. 2	Sect. 3	Unit	Growth
A. Structure	%	%	%	%	%	%
B. Narratives						
C. Features			xxxxxxx			
Total						